Contents

Empowerment, Assessment, Care Management

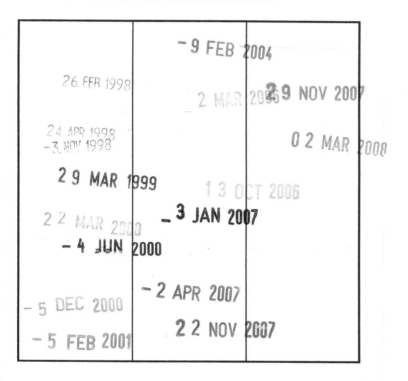

National Institute for Social Work

Practice and Development Exchange

London: HMSO

ISBN 0 11 321555 X

Further information regarding this and other NISW titles may be obtained from:

National Institute for Social Work
5 Tavistock Place
London
WC1H 9SS

Telephone: 071 387 9681

Preface

Empowering Users to Make Choices: Assessment, Care Management and the Skilled Worker was commissioned by the Department of Health (DoH) to:

1   Look at the interactional skills required by social services (and other) staff carrying out assessments and care management tasks.

2   Specifically, to describe how the worker should behave to ensure that the user is empowered by the process sufficiently to participate to the maximum degree possible in the choice to be made about how his/her needs are to be addressed.

3   To show how those making assessments and managing cases can involve members of the user's social networks to negotiate and sustain arrangements which integrate resources from the statutory and independent sectors with the help given through family and/or neighbourhood networks.

This work was carried out at the same time as a parallel working party was engaged in reviewing research on community-based practice to identify implications for the implementation of the NHS and Community Care and the Children Acts. Detailed references to some of the issues discussed here are to be found in that report, *Negotiating Care in the Community: The implications of research findings on community based practice for the implementation of the NHS and Community Care and the Children Acts* (Smale et al, 1992). The two publications should be read together.

However it is also necessary to identify many of the core skills required for assessment and care management to be able to carry out effective consultations. The report begins with a discussion of this issue and some principles underlying empowerment, assessment and care management drawn from our experience of developing community-based practice in partnership with local people: National Institute for Social Work (NISW) Practice and Development Exchange (PADE)'s Community Social Work Exchange funded by the DoH, and the Social Work in Partnership project at Sheffield and Bradford Universities (SWIP) funded by the Joseph Rowntree Foundation.

Our brief was to focus on the principles and skills required by professionals to engage appropriately in face-to-face contact with members of the public in making assessments and managing care, not on consultations between users and professionals to plan services either at the area team or local authority level. Our view is that it is impossible and undesirable to make a clear cut distinction between these two levels; that the skills outlined here will be relevant to the areas of practice and management that overlap. However, further work needs to be done on these issues, as it does on the development of programmes for supporting service users.

Identifying principles and skills is a first step in a more comprehensive process including drawing up practice guides at a local level in partnership with local people and organisations.

Part One addresses a framework for empowering people participating in the process of assessment and care management, the principles underlying forming partnerships with people, identifying who needs to be approached and looks at how care management can be defined and related to empowerment.

Part Two describes the core skills identified in the research and development literature on community-based approaches to social work practice and service delivery, work published by the Race Equality Unit on the Black perspective on community care, outcome research in "helping relationships" including social work practice, counselling, psychotherapy, groupwork, and family therapy, and the Social Work in Partnership Project.

Membership of the Group

Nina Biehal, University of Leeds
Peter Marsh, University of Sheffield
Gerald Smale, National Institute for Social Work, London
Graham Tuson, University of Southampton

Acknowledgements

This work was supported by the Social Services Inspectorate of the Department of Health. We would like to thank all the people, whether "professional" or not, who have participated in the Community Social Work Exchange and the Social Work in Partnership Project. Roy Pearson provided invaluable support and encouragement and we are grateful for the valuable comments and criticisms we received from Daphne Statham, Adele Jones, Barbara Hearn, Liz Timms, Mike Wardle, Mary Greenwood, Roger Winter, and members of their teams. The patient efforts of Nancy Dunlop were essential throughout and Margaret Hogan's editorial skills have greatly improved on our efforts.

PART ONE

Introduction

The Dilemma of Writing about User Participation, and the Scope of the Report

The philosophy of partnership

To be consistent with the philosophy of partnership we should identify how professionals should conduct assessments and "manage care" by involving the people who receive services and their carers from across the whole spectrum of people involved. Special efforts will have to be made to include those who are typically under-represented or not heard.

Hearing the voice of service users

But to engage in consultation with users about how to assess their needs raises a chicken and egg problem. To consult with "service users" and "carers" so that professionals "hear" what they really say, and not what the professionals expect them to say, assumes that those conducting the consultation know how to behave appropriately when doing so, specifically that they know how to listen and talk in the right languages to communicate with people dependent upon others for their care, their carers and the other people in the community who are involved. The "chicken and egg" problem is that to consult effectively with people in the community about the knowledge and skills necess- ary for an empowering approach to assessment and care management **requires** that the staff involved in such consul- tations already have the necessary know-how and skills. Such consultative processes are essentially the same as the consultative processes required for assessment and care management themselves.

A further problem has to be confronted if carers and users involved in community care are to be empowered. A representa- tive group of people dependent upon others and their carers would, by definition, speak for people like themselves at a par- ticular point in time, discuss the issues as they see them and attempt to resolve the problems that they anticipate. This is the essential process that departments and agencies should go through when planning their services to build up a general pic- ture of people's needs and the kinds of assessment and care man- agement that they want to participate in. Professionals have to avoid the danger that generalisations arrived at through these consultations will turn into a sophisticated stereotyping process if simplistically applied at the operational face-to-face level. It is necessary to be aware of shared concerns and the significant cultural variations of class, ethnicity and local communities while at the same time recognising difference and diversity in individuals and the idiosyncratic nature of social networks.

Reinventing practice

To empower users, carers and the other people they work with and to respond to the unique circumstances that confront them on a day by day basis, professionals have to **reinvent** their practice and their perception of particular problems and solutions in each different social situation that they find themselves in. This involves an approach to practice based on a sound understanding of the **basic principles** that underlie the processes of empowerment and the application of **skills** of engaging **with** people to jointly assess situations and negotiate who can do what to support whom. Workers have to "improvise" in harmony with the other "players" on the day, based on underlying principles, in the same way as musicians will base their playing on a chord sequence. It is wise to start with a negotiation about the key that the tune will be played in and be prepared to change the chord sequence when necessary.

Professional practice and general principles

Preparing workers to engage in assessment and care management with citizens cannot be done by managers drawing up detailed procedures and lists of questions. Whitehead's statement about higher education is particularly relevant to practice. The word "student" is easily replaced by "professional", and for "text book" read "procedures manual":

> "Whatever be the detail with which you cram your student, the chance of their meeting in after-life exactly that detail is almost infinitesimal: and if they do meet it, they will probably have forgotten what you taught them about it. The really useful training yields a comprehension of a few general principles with thorough grounding in the way they apply to a variety of concrete details. In subsequent practice, people will have forgotten your particular details; but they will remember by an unconscious common sense how to apply principles to immediate circumstances. Your learning is useless to you till you have lost your text book, burnt your lecture notes, and forgotten the minute detail that you learnt for the examination." (Whitehead, 1929 p.41; gender adjustments made to the text)

Needs, choice and power

It is a basic assumption that people can get the service they want, and one they would agree meets their needs without having been empowered; just as sometimes we get the weather we want. Indeed it is possible to be rendered powerless by the process. It is also the case that people can have as much power as it is possible for a person to have and still not get what they desire or need. Can anybody have the power to be sure of being cared for because others care about them?

Who are the "professionals"

Throughout we refer to "the professional". The term is used here in the sense that some footballers are "professional", meaning that they are paid, that their training and skill makes them fitter and more consistent than amateurs who can and do play. This is of course not always true, even of footballers. Professionals are also expected to conduct themselves in certain ways to meet ethical standards to protect those they serve and so as not to "bring the game into disrepute". By this definition, a home-help is as much a professional as a Dip.S.W. qualified social worker (Smale and Tuson, 1988). Hence the term "social work" is used in a way which is inclusive of the actions of staff who, although they may not be "social workers", are engaged in "the social work process".

The social services supermarket

Imagine turning up at the supermarket to be met by an "assessor", or "gatekeeper of resources", perhaps called a "shopping manager". On entering the shop to acquire your package of goods, or perhaps the shopping manager visits you because somebody has told them you need some groceries but cannot go out, this person explains that their job is to work with you to identify your needs, and to form an opinion of what kind of package of goods you need and what resources can be called upon to obtain them. The shopping manager also explains that this particular supermarket no longer provides many "goods" themselves but the manager will contract with a supplier who does.

Self-service customers

The vast majority of people, probably like yourself until now, will not come to the Social Services Supermarket to meet their needs: they will serve themselves or be "served" by the relatives, friends and neighbours who provide the bulk of care in the community. Relatively few people call upon the social services for support: of the 6 million carers supporting a dependent person in the community only 6% received regular visits from social workers, 23% home-helps, 7% meals-on-wheels (Green, 1988). More might well call if they knew what services were on offer, or even if they had any idea that there was help available for people in their situation.

There will be people who can go right past you and buy the goods they choose, but they are spending their own money, not state resources administered by social services and social work departments.

Helping the customers

Good, trustworthy sales staff have a vital role to play in a shop that sells technically sophisticated or highly specialised goods that the customer knows little about. Staff concerned with long term relationships and not just quick sales can also be helpful sources of information about who can supply goods when they cannot, while the "street corner" shopkeeper can play a vital role in community networks. These people do more than package goods. In the ordinary supermarket consumers normally have the power to hold back their money and to some extent the protection of consumer groups and legislation. Crucial questions facing social services staff attempting to perform this delicate task include:

- how can they responsibly account for their use of state resources which they have the responsibility to "gatekeep", and empower those people receiving services?

- how can they carry out assessments and deliver, or make sure that somebody else delivers a service so that the customers exercise real choice?

- how can we, the professionals in social services, conduct ourselves so that people are "empowered" and not made more powerless by having to go through the process of "professional help", of having their "needs assessed" and their "care managed"?

Who are the customers?

A simple way of giving those who recognise that they need a service the power to become customers, is to give them the financial resources and information to gain direct access to the services they want. In community care this simple solution is complicated by confusion over identifying who the customer is. Is the service offered to a dependent person just for them, or is the carer, who is partially or completely relieved of their task as a result, also a customer? Many people come into this category, particularly when the "dependent" person's behaviour causes concern: for example, relatives and neighbours who are relieved of anxiety, the hospital doctor whose beds are freed, the policy makers whose responsibilities are discharged. The concerns of these people partly explain why two thirds of the elderly people in residential care become residents against their wishes (Neill et al, 1988; Sinclair et al, 1990).

Who can make choices?

Any approach to "giving people choice", short of enabling them to buy the services they require, obtain them as a right, or develop them through their personal relationships, runs the risk of maintaining or even increasing people's powerlessness. **There has to be a good reason for not allowing people to be their own care manager.** Carers typically manage the care of the dependent person they care for, sharing the responsibility with them in varying degrees. Empowering citizens to live as independent a life as possible cannot be achieved by diminishing these responsibilities. The task can be shared by contributing social services resources and negotiating additional help from others, but the professional should not attempt to control, or take responsibility for the whole "package of care", only for their contribution to it. All those who are going to participate in providing and receiving care should participate in the decisions about who should do what to support whom, including the allocation of specific resources, as much as possible.

Gatekeeping without taking over

Does old age or physical disability make people unable to fully participate in these decisions, or being without their own money mean they are incapable of managing it? The challenge confronting professionals in social services departments is to "gatekeep" the available resources without retaining all the power to spend it themselves. Social services professionals will have to resolve these issues. They will surface when making assessments. It is when doing these assessments that workers will routinely confront issues of empowerment. Will they share everything with the people they are working with?

Information experience and choice

Being a customer with money in your pocket is not an insurance against powerlessness. It is difficult for users to make real choices when their past experience of using social services is limited (Willcocks et al, 1982). There is always the tendency for "people to want what they know rather than know what they want" (Morrison, 1988). Information about the availability of services as a source of power is well documented (Berry, 1990; SSI, 1987; Wagner, 1988; Sinclair et al, 1990) and is the subject of the DoH/SSI publication *Getting the Message Across* (1991). Research on communication in health care emphasises the difficulties that professionals have in conveying even simple information to patients; for example Higbee et al (1982) show how even single item prescription information is often not recalled.

Information about social services is of great importance because the services are often crucial to the user's welfare and because of the wide imbalance in the amount of information possessed by providers and consumers. People need information about goals and objectives, about the standards of service authorities aim to provide and the standards achieved; about their rights to a service and their responsibilities in using them; about the way authorities are structured and the decision-making process; about why decisions are taken and about what those decisions actually are (Potter, 1988).

Ensuring choice is available

Croft and Beresford (1990) studied more than eighty initiatives to increase people's choice and involvement in social services and point out that:
> "The extent to which people have a say in services depends more on the efforts made to ensure it than the particular source of service supply. Purchase of service does not necessarily bring with it control of service. Existing initiatives suggest that just changing the service supplier or moving to a mixed economy of care won't necessarily offer people more choice and say in services. Instead arrangements must be made to provide it." (Croft and Beresford, 1990 p.13).

They stress that people will need to be prepared and supported to service their choice. This is particularly true of those participating in planning processes. Just as this report focuses on the skills of professionals, so we need to identify the development needs of their partners. Parent governors are given free training to equip them for their role and similar support will be required by service users contributing to community care planning.

Partnership between Citizens or Expert-Client Relationships?

Workers can either "play a crucial role" in understanding the problems of the "client" or work alongside the person who has been identified as "the client" and the other significant people in the situation, to arrive at a mutual understanding of the problem and negotiate who might do what to help. Both approaches may end up with the person getting what they want; or not, if resources are not available. The difference is in how power is used and its impact on the service user. Only the latter will empower the citizen to be fully involved as an equal partner in a process of negotiating the nature of "their problem" and its possible "solutions" through an appropriate "tailor-made package of care". These two approaches reflect two models of assessment: the former we call the **Questioning** model, the latter we call the **Exchange** model. A third approach, the **Procedural** model, a variation of the Questioning model, is also described below.

In the Questioning model the professional is assumed to be the expert in identifying need. In the Procedural model, a variation of the Questioning model, it is assumed that the managers drawing up guidelines for workers have expertise in setting the criteria for resource allocation. To this extent they are the experts in how problems should be managed and resources allocated. In the Exchange model, it is assumed that the "clients" and other people in the situation, and the professional, all have equally valid perceptions of the problems and can contribute to their solution or perpetuation.

The distinction between these approaches can be illustrated with a discussion of a situation which involves five people: the "client", the "carer", the "carer's partner", the "referrer" and the "assessor-care manager" (referred to here as the "professional"). Often more people will, and should, be involved.

Our example focuses on Mrs Smith, her daughter Rose, and son-in-law Tom. Mrs Smith is in hospital following a fall. She is referred for residential accommodation by a hospital doctor who has spoken to Rose. Rose and Tom feel they cannot have her home. An assessment is called for.

There are many ways of approaching this. We have assumed that the professional will see *all* the people involved as "the unit of assessment", and not just the individuals, Mrs Smith and the "carer", Rose.

Figs I and II illustrate the Questioning and Exchange models for engaging with these people to "assess" their situation and begin to negotiate a package of care.

Fig I: The Questioning Model (*Smale, 1991*)

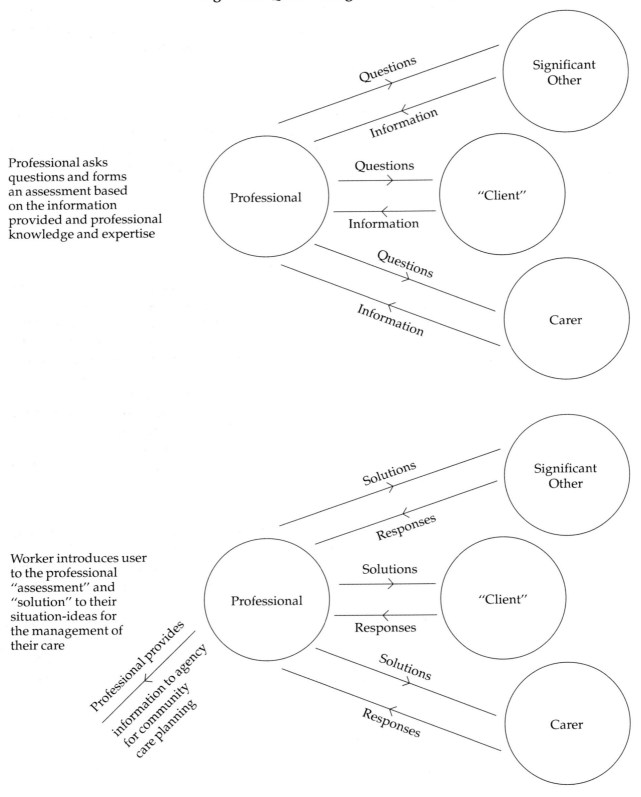

Professional asks questions and forms an assessment based on the information provided and professional knowledge and expertise

Worker introduces user to the professional "assessment" and "solution" to their situation-ideas for the management of their care

The Questioning model	In the Questioning model a professional gathers information from Mrs Smith, the "client", and Rose her "carer", forms an assessment of their needs or problems and then works on a solution. In this scenario the worker's behaviour is dominated by asking questions, listening to and processing the answers, using the information gained to form "an assessment", perhaps by filling in an "assessment form", to formulate the requirements of a future package of care. The questions reflect the worker's agenda, not other people's. Enshrined in the questions asked will be implicit or explicit criteria or perceptions of the problems that people like Mrs Smith have, and a view of the resources available to meet them.
Limitations	In this model it is often assumed that questions can be answered in a straightforward manner, or that the professional is able to accurately interpret what Mrs Smith really wants even when she cannot or does not express it. The complexities of communication across cultural and other boundaries, such as race, ethnicity as defined by professionals, gender, class, disability or professional reference group and organisational allegiance, tend to be underestimated or even ignored.
Beyond identifying "need"	An "accurate professional assessment" may be enough to identify "need", but it is not enough if goals include increasing the choices of the people involved, maintaining independence and maximising people's potential. Additional skills are needed for work *with* people that empowers them to have as much control over their lives as possible, and specifically enables them to exercise choice in how their needs may be met. *Caring for People* (DoH, 1989) and the subsequent guidelines make it clear that the intention is that it should be a needs-led assessment not a service-led exercise: an assessment of what the people in the situation want and need and not "how can they be fitted into existing provision".
The Exchange model	In the alternative Exchange model, the professional concentrates on an exchange of information between themselves and Mrs Smith, Rose, Tom and others. The question and answer pattern of behaviour will be avoided. The kind of information that is likely to come out of this sort of assessment will be different as are the underlying principles of the "process". The professional works to engage with all three people involved, and others where relevant, including other professionals. Meetings may be with all three people together or in series; their participation is negotiable.

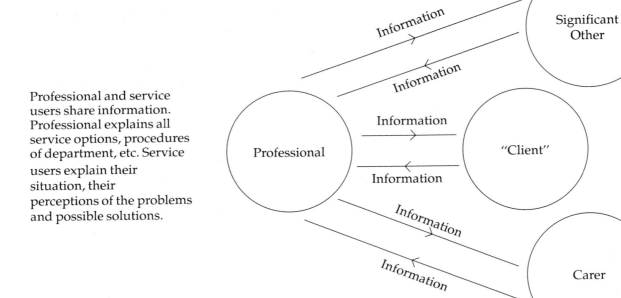

Professional and service
users share information.
Professional explains all
service options, procedures
of department, etc. Service
users explain their
situation, their
perceptions of the problems
and possible solutions.

Professional and service
users and others arrive at
a mutual understanding of
problems, their possible
solutions or management

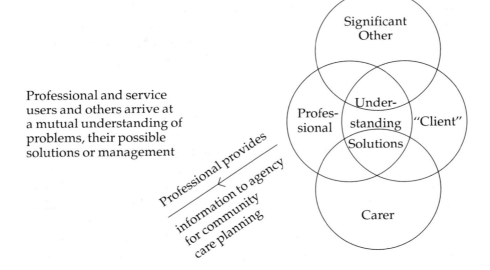

The behaviour of the professional is crucial in establishing the respect and trust of the others and will vary over time. Perceptions of the situation, its problems, availability of resources and the need for more, are shared. A definition of the "problems" and their resolution or management are arrived at as much through the initiative of Mrs Smith, Rose or Tom as by the professional. More will be said of the skills required to engage in this kind of relationship in Part Two.

In the Exchange model two or more people come together and arrive at a mutual understanding of the nature of the problem, its solution or management, through the interaction between them. Typically the professional will not lead the content of the dialogue because he or she will not know any more, if as much, as the other people about the situation, its problems, or what existing resources could contribute to "the solution", i.e. the potential components of a "package of care". The professional follows or tracks what the other people say and communicate. To lead is to assume that the professional knows where to go, and often this will be straight to a service-led response.

Levels and languages of communication

The communication of what people need and want is very complicated and has to include an exploration of, and take into account, the different assumptions of the two or more people involved, the different languages that they use, think and feel in, and the different levels of communication that exist.

Communication across ethnic, racial, class, gender, professional, or other cultural boundaries needs particular care if preconceived assumptions and prejudices are not going to lead to misunderstanding or worse. Interpreters should be able to demonstrate the communication skills outlined below in both languages. It is not sufficient to turn to anybody who can translate only the words.

Language, expectations and partnership

People have their own ideas, beliefs and knowledge; they are not passive or neutral receivers waiting for messages. In practice communicators enter into dialogues with people who interpret messages in accordance with their own assumptions and beliefs, which may or may not be the same as the communicators. Those sending communications may be clear about what they intend to say, but they should never prejudge what the other person receives. In their "own minds" those receiving a message will hear what the message means to them, they will understand or not, agree or disagree with the communication, and then react, which may or may not be overtly consistent with what they think. We are reminded of the young offender who said to his social worker, "I have decided to go straight". The curious worker asked why; at which the young man swore and said, "Don't you want me to go straight?". In his world you are only asked such a question by a person in authority when you have done something wrong; in her world it was a "neutral" question.

People are not empowered by professionals who assume an all encompassing expert role. A recognition of who is expert in what is central to collaboration and so to the way in which the relationship between these people will develop and whether **partnerships** are formed between two or more people, or just role relationships between "professionals" and "clients".

The theoretical basis

The theory underlying the Exchange model is supported by consumer studies and outcome research into helping relationships in social work, health care, counselling, psychotherapy, groupwork and family therapy relationships, referenced in Part Two; research into adult learning and the transfer of new ways of solving problems; and into the transfer of innovations.

Communication as convergence

It is often assumed that new solutions to problems are disseminated by information passing from an "expert", or from the policy makers at the top of an organisation, to others, who are either open to help, information, advice or instruction, or "resistant" to change. This view does not fit the growing mass of research into the diffusion of innovations. After reviewing more than 1300 studies, Rogers (1983) has developed a model for understanding the processes of diffusion. He concluded that:

> "Communication is a process in which participants create and share information with one another in order to reach a mutual understanding. This definition implies that communication is a process of convergence (or divergence) as two or more individuals exchange information in order to move toward each other (or apart) in the meanings that they ascribe to certain events. We think of communication as a two-way process of convergence, rather than a one-way, linear act in which one individual seeks to transfer a message to another (Rogers and Kincaid, 1981)." (Rogers, 1983)

This argument has much in common with the body of knowledge built up on adult learning. Paulo Freire's work on adult literacy and education is recognised as having wide relevance (Freire, 1972; Shaull, 1972). Criticising orthodox approaches to education where the teacher relates to students as if the latter were "receptacles to be filled by the teacher", Freire points out that:

> "Instead of communicating, the teacher issues communiques and 'makes deposits' which the students patiently receive, memorise, and repeat. This is the 'banking' concept of education, in which the scope of action allowed to the students extends only as far as receiving, filing, and storing the deposits."

However, Freire argues that:

> "Knowledge emerges only through invention and re-invention, through the restless, impatient, continuing, hopeful inquiry men (sic) pursue in the world, with the world, and with each other." (Friere, 1972 pp.45, 46).

Collaborative working relationships	Changes in attitude such as these are also being developed within health care. Meichenbaum and Turk (1987) in their summary of the research on patient adherence to therapeutic regimes express it in the following way:

> "Rather than the Health Care Professional's assuming the role of the 'expert' who dispenses information and recommendations, increased levels of adherence may be dependent upon *a more collaborative working relationship*" (p.54; their italics).

Who is the expert?	**People are, and always will be the expert on themselves** (Bricker-Jenkins, 1990; Smale et al, 1988): their situation, their relationships, what they want and need. No matter how easy or difficult it is for the professional to communicate with people, the people always bring their expertise about themselves to the assessment and subsequent "management" of their care. They will also bring a certain degree of control over their own behaviour that professionals will never have and so be able to influence the viability of the present and future relationships that underpin a "package of care".

Redefining "professional" expertise	We need a redefinition of the expertise required by "professionals" if "partnership" with people and full participation in choice is to be the goal of the way in which assessments are carried out. This includes expertise in the **process** of assessments involving complex negotiations:

- expertise in facilitating people's attempts to articulate and so identify their own needs and clarify what they want.

- sensitivity to language, cultural, racial and gender differences.

- the ability to help people through major transitions involving loss. Assessments will often take place at times of great stress, through loss of a partner or some physical capacity, or some other change that has precipitated referral. At these times any person intervening to help make decisions about major issues, decisions which are themselves often major transitions in people's lives, will need skills and knowledge typically associated with counselling.

- the ability to negotiate and conciliate between people who have different perceptions, values, attitudes, expectations, wants and needs. Many of the situations being assessed contain the conflicting needs of several people whose relationships have formed over many years. Negotiating who can and will do what to support whom under these circumstances and within inevitable resource constraints will require knowledge and skills associated with some approaches to family therapy and similar complex social interventions.

Exchanging information	Professionals are in a pivotal position in the transfer of information between the public and the agency. Thus they will need to be able to:

- provide information to citizens and share expertise in the ways of the personal social services system, to inform people of possible alternative choices;

- provide information for social care planning to their own and other agencies and to act as an advocate for the needs of citizens.

The Exchange model recognises that there will be many sources of information, only one of which is the product of direct questions by the worker. If they know their community well the worker may already have a great deal of information about the general circumstances of the person. Although they will often not have had direct contact with the particular person, they may have had some contact with neighbours or others in the immediate vicinity. If such information about the social situation is not known then the worker will set about getting it. We will see below that, in the relationship with Mrs Smith, Rose and Tom, the worker will draw on this information as much as she will apply her skills to "hear" what they say, make implications about their situation and negotiate how they might be helped.

Identifying relationships between people

The assessor should also be expert in identifying the relationships between people. This includes understanding how their behaviour supports the current situation, and how this may be changed to support a different pattern of relationships so that the problem can be managed differently, or the problem resolved in the case of one or more people's "behaviour" being the reason for referral to social work or social services. In short, professionals need to be able to recognise, understand and intervene in the patterns of relationships that precipitate and perpetuate social problems. (Smale et al, 1988)

All people have expertise in these areas, some more than others. It is essential that the professional recognises that they do not start with a monopoly of this knowledge and that they should share what they have with all the other people involved. An essential part of their responsibility is to add to, but keep out of the way of others exercising their own social problem solving skills.

The "third party" perspective

Citizens are expert in themselves and their relationships as they see them from inside their situation. A professional, marginal to these relationships, may be able to contribute a valuable "third party" perspective common in many forms of conciliation and negotiation. Thus the assessor should also be expert in:

- identifying the relationships between people, how their behaviour supports current relationships, and how this may be changed to support a different set of behaviours so that the problem can be managed differently, or the problem resolved in the case of people's "behaviour" being the reason for referral to social work or social services;

- recognising, understanding and intervening in the patterns of relationships between individuals and between groups and organisations that precipitate and perpetuate social problems. (Smale et al, 1988).

The skills involved in this redefinition of the expertise required by professionals are discussed further in Part Two of this report. Clearly professionals undertaking such work will need to be well supervised, not only because of their accountability to the agency as gatekeepers of resources, but also to enable them to maintain their "third party position" in complex negotiations, and to support them in work which will often make acute emotional demands.

The Questioning and Exchange Models of Assessment

*Differing
assumptions and
responsibility*

There is a crucial difference in the assumptions of the Questioning and Exchange models of assessment (see Fig III). In the first it is assumed that the worker is an expert in people, or their problems, or both. In the second it is assumed that all people are expert in their own problems and that there is no reason to assume that the worker will or should ever know more about people and their problems than they do themselves, and certainly not before they do.

Both models assume the worker brings expertise in relating to people, knowledge about the "welfare system", and skills in problem solving and developing the mix of different people's efforts and other resources, currently referred to as "packages of care".

In the Questioning model it is assumed that the worker will exercise this knowledge and skill to form an assessment, identify people's needs and the resources that are required to meet them, and, where the assessor and care manager are the same person, act as broker to secure an appropriate package of care. The professional is responsible for making an accurate assessment of need and taking the appropriate action.

The Exchange model emphasises expertise in **the process of problem solving; the ability to work towards a mutual understanding of "the problem" with all the major actors.** The process involves working with people to understand their differing perceptions and interests and to arrive at a compromise. This involves negotiating with a range of people—from the dependent person, their immediate carers and other people in the community, to service providers from different agencies and professions. **Instead of the worker making "an assessment"** and organising care and support for people, which carries the implicit assumption of control, **the worker negotiates to get agreement about who should do what for whom.**

The worker is responsible for conducting the negotiations and the agency's contribution to the situation. Responsibility for arriving at the best possible arrangements for the care of the people involved, or for the best obtainable resolution of the problem, within the constraints of available resources, is shared with others as it is dependent upon the willingness and ability of other participants to contribute. In this sense the professional can never be responsible for the whole "package of care". Each participant is responsible for their contribution, or lack of it.

The Questioning model and individual needs

The goal of the Questioning model is legitimate in some contexts, often difficult but relatively simple. It is to obtain a professional assessment of the best possible package of care to meet the needs of the person assessed, as defined by the professional, leading to service delivery, assuming resources are available.

The Questioning model has advantages for the agency; it is relatively quick and straightforward. It tends to focus on **the dependency needs of the individual**. It will tend to ignore the resources actually or potentially available in the social situation and underestimate the control that other people have over them.

The Exchange model and "choice"

The goal of the Exchange model is also legitimate, always difficult and relatively complex. It is to obtain the best possible arrangements for care as identified by the major parties so that people can continue to live "as normal a life as possible", and in the **process**, "achieve maximum possible independence" and have "a greater individual say in how they live their lives and the services they need to help them do so"; that is, be empowered to exercise "choice". The limitations of resources will be taken into account in this process and arrangements made even if it is acknowledged that more resources could greatly improve the situation for some or all of the participants. (All quotes from *Caring for People* DoH, 1989.)

Establishing partnerships

The Exchange model typically includes more people and takes longer. It focuses on the dependency needs of the service user and others, **their various perceptions of the alternative solutions and the dependability of all the people in the situation.** It has advantages for the agency by establishing partnerships with the resources normally mobilised to provide care in the community. It has advantages for "dependent" people, their carers and the other people involved: it values their contribution and gives them greater say in the management of services additional to their own efforts.

Fig III: The Questioning and Exchange Models. *The Assumptions Compared*

THE QUESTIONING MODEL	THE EXCHANGE MODEL
Assumes the worker:	Assumes that people:
• is expert in people, their problems and needs;	• are expert in themselves.
• exercises knowledge and skill to form "their" assessment, identify people's needs;	Assumes that the worker:
• identifies resources required;	• has expertise in the **process** of problem solving with others;
• takes responsibility for making an accurate assessment of need and taking appropriate action.	• understands and shares perceptions of problems and their management;
	• gets agreement about who will do what to support whom;
	• takes responsibility for arriving at the optimum resolution of problems within the constraints of available resources and the willingness of participants to contribute.

Both models assume the worker brings expertise in relating to people, knowledge about the "welfare system", and skills in problem solving and developing "packages of care".

Criteria for eligibility

The Questioning model assumes that the assessors' judgments and actions are relatively independent of their agency and/or service providers. It is often assumed that their behaviour is informed by implicit or explicit criteria based on "professional" knowledge. Such professional "autonomy" may not exist or be very limited. Marsh and Fisher's (1992) work on "partnership in practice" illustrates how staff get pulled into an administrative mode even where there is no organisational demand to do so. However, many workers will operate within given agency guidelines and criteria for the allocation of scarce resources and will be expected to gather specific information as a basis for judgments. This is illustrated by the third model, the Procedural model (Fig IV). In this the goal of the assessment is to gather information to see if the client "fits", or meets, certain criteria that will "make them eligible for services". Those defining the criteria for eligibility, in effect pre-allocating services for generally identified need, make the judgment as to what sort of person should get which resources. The worker's task is to identify the specific people who match the appropriate degree of need defined within the categories of service available and to exclude those not eligible.

Gathering information for resource allocation

In this model the worker will complete a form with, or without, the "client", "carer", parent or other significant person. Including the citizen in this process may be good manners but it does not constitute empowering them to make choices about the arrangements to be made for their care or that of their relatives, friends or neighbours. Questions are asked and/or information gathered to answer each of the questions deemed relevant by those setting criteria for resource allocation. What is, and is not, a relevant question is judged by those laying down the procedures and policy of the agency reflected in the questions. The information typically sought attempts to:

- identify a particular level of dependency, that is to categorise the "client", (without always seeking a map of who does, or could meet these dependency needs and without describing the social situation within which a person, or people have been identified as "in need");

- define the nature of the client's needs in the terms that services are offered, that is whether the client's needs make them eligible for services actually or potentially available;

- gather information required for agency statistics to aid service planning (community care plans).

Fig IV: The Procedural Model (*Smale, 1991*)

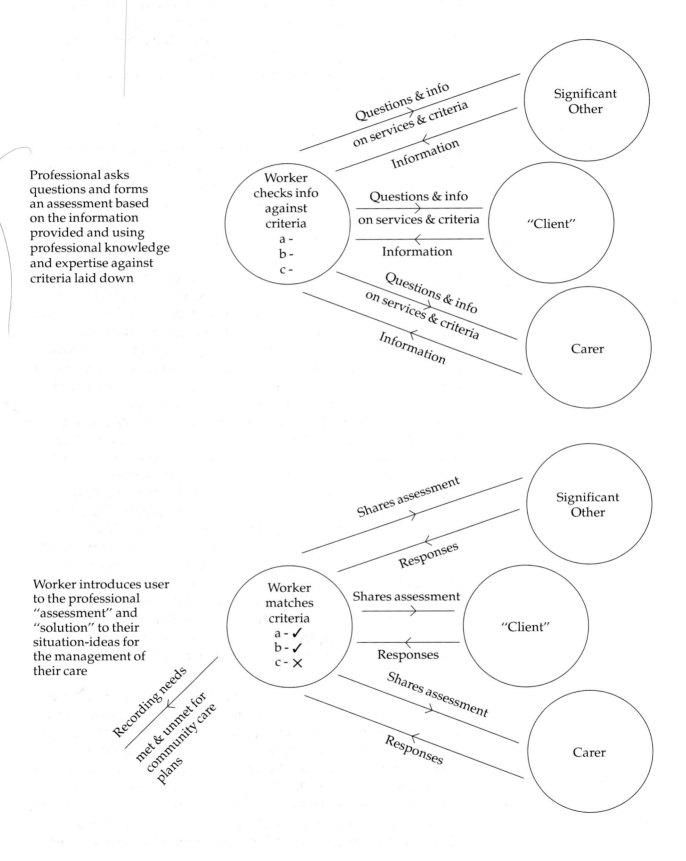

Professional asks questions and forms an assessment based on the information provided and using professional knowledge and expertise against criteria laid down

Worker introduces user to the professional "assessment" and "solution" to their situation-ideas for the management of their care

Definitions of service and perceptions of problems

The "clients'" definitions of their problems, or that of others, may or may not be included. It is certainly very difficult to match the explicit or implicit agenda of such forms to the infinite variety of ways in which different people from very different backgrounds and assumptions will see their problems and their potential solutions. Consumer studies and research on services for minority ethnic groups consistently demonstrate that current definitions of service do not fit people's own perception of their problems. Often such definitions will be hard to match against specific criteria.

Whose agenda?

The agenda is set, not by worker or client, but by those who draw up the forms, and where the questions require specific answers about needs related to potential services, the process will be service-driven rather than needs-driven. Even if the "clients" get what they want, they are not "empowered" by the process. They do not make choices, nor does the worker, beyond interpreting how the information is used.

In this model the agenda is set by the agency. The agency remains central to the definition of problems and the range of available solutions. It is also the case that many workers will only see the agency, or other professionals, as resources or service providers. The clients may or may not get what they want and/or need. The worker may or may not judge that the clients' needs have been met. But the worker's judgment, beyond interpreting information and deciding on how to fill in the form, is not required. In this model neither the worker, nor the client or any other interviewee, are empowered by the process. The worker has little room to manoeuvre except in interpreting how to put questions and how to record the answers. The worker's responsibility is for the authority delegated to them to make judgments, within the agenda set by those designing the form and the decisions made by those deciding on eligibility. The worker is responsible for collecting the information appropriately, and maybe for matching people to the criteria and allocating resources accordingly. Managers are responsible for the allocation of services to meet need within resource constraints placed upon them. People in the community are responsible for providing information and accepting the decisions made, using complaints procedures to challenge them when they are aggrieved.

The 'helpful' worker problem

One problem confronting those managing people operating the Procedural model lies in the private nature of assessment activity and the tendency for workers, particularly sensitive, caring ones, to identify with the people who are experiencing problems. It is understandable if "helpful" workers try to help the client to meet the criteria that will enable them to get what people say they need, and what the workers judge they need, even if they do not actually meet management criteria, and even if in so doing the client has a more pathological label attached to them for being identified as "more needy". We can expect a significant increase in the number of people "judged" to be in need of residential care if "danger of admission to residential care" becomes the criteria for receiving day and domiciliary services.

Practical advantages of the Procedural model

The goal of the Procedural model is, in some contexts, legitimate. It is to provide a cost effective way of identifying the clients who are eligible for available services. Such procedures, typically, also strive toward the equitable allocation of scarce resources to people meeting specific criteria.

The Procedural model is probably the simplest and quickest and, in this sense, the most practical approach. Staff can be trained to do it and do not have to be educated to make judgments. It also has the advantage of being controlled by managers, and can easily be responsive to changes in policy about resource allocation through changing the criteria without changing the format of interviews or departmental forms used.

Worker/manager expertise

In this approach the worker is expert in gathering information, and acts as the agent of the manager who is the expert in identifying how resources should be allocated to tackle problems. This expertise is reflected in decisions about resource allocation, on the application of policy about who should get what resource. It is also present in defining the criteria that should be applied; this involves making judgments about the nature of the problems that people have and the use to be made of available resources.

Combining the three models

Practitioners and managers introduced to these models have sometimes pointed out that they want to apply a little of all of them. **It should be clear that some dimensions of each exclude the application of others.** It is necessary to be clear what the worker, and so the agency, intends to achieve. If the major goal is to allocate some resources to particular people using briefly trained staff, then the Procedural model is the most practical but it will not empower all participants to participate in the complex choices to be made. If the decision on who should get what is to rest on the professional judgment of need then the Questioning model can be used, but it should be recognised that the questions are designed to help the worker, not the user, understand the situation and come to a conclusion. Discussing this conclusion with other participants does not add up to empowerment. **The Exchange model is designed to share decision making** between all parties; to negotiate who can do what for whom and **to maximise people's choices.**

If parts of all three models are used, we suggest it is clear to citizens that much of the information gathered is **to help the professional and the agency exercise their choice and make their decisions** which may, or may not, help them. In situations where social control, the minimisation of risk to the client and others, is a major concern, such an approach is often seen as legitimate. In our experience it is usually more effective to start with the approach of the Exchange model. This has the advantage of the worker giving a full explanation of their position and that of the agency. It is also much more difficult to get out of the pattern of questions and answers, than it is to gather specific information after an exchange of perceptions about the current problems and their potential solution. The mixed approach will require workers to have a "good enough" level of the skills outlined in Part Two.

Assessment of "Individuals" or "Social Situations"?

"The Government acknowledges that the great bulk of community care is provided by friends, family and neighbours." (*Caring for People* DoH, 1989 1.9.)

Who normally cares?

In Britain there are some 6 million unpaid carers of people other than children, of whom 1.4 million devote over twenty hours per week to caring, and a quarter have looked after a dependent person for at least ten years. Nearly two thirds of carers, 3.7 million, carry the main responsibility for the care of a dependent person, either alone or jointly with someone else, and so act as a "care manager" as well as direct service provider.

It is common for carers to feel that they have been left, even abandoned, to support the dependent person on their own. About one quarter of carers report that no-one else helps. Only about one half of carers have dependents who receive regular visits from health or social services or from voluntary groups. "Regular" is defined as "at least once per month". Of these visitors, 43% were health professionals while only 6% were social workers, 23% home-helps, 7% meals-on-wheels and 4% voluntary workers (Green, 1988).

Working in partnership

It is clear that people are **normally** cared for in our community by their relatives, friends or neighbours. Barclay (1982), *Scottish Health Authorities Review of Priorities for the Eighties and Nineties* (1984), Griffiths (1988) and *Caring for People* (1989) all underlined the fact that social workers and other members of the caring professions have a crucial part to play, but they also need to recognise that they are peripheral to the bulk of care in the community. It is equally obvious that social services play little or no part in the upbringing of the great majority of children.

The essence of empowerment, of working in partnership, is to work **with** these people, not to take over what responsibility or control that they do have, but to bring new resources to their situation to build on and add to what they do and the choice they have in how care in the community works for them.

The Focus of Attention and the Need for Reform

Empowering service users and carers

The emphasis on choice, independence, and users and carers having more say in how they live their lives and the services they need to help them to do so, underlies the need to focus on empowerment. The goals of achieving maximum possible independence, potential, and enabling people to live as normal a life as possible, underlies the need to recognise the significance of the social situation.

The significance of the social situation

A person can be totally isolated and have many unmet needs, but as soon as it is said that "something should be done" others become involved. **It is impossible for a person to be dependent on their own.** The very word assumes that more than one person exists. **The question "what does this person need?" is inseparable from "who is doing what for whom?" and "who could do what to help?"** For services to be provided to those who are dependent upon others is then a service to those upon whom they might have depended. Professional services are essential because some people do not have dependable people in their lives either to provide support or to organise it, or because the conflicts in perception or interests cause problems for participants and because many carers are left to cope with the responsibility and tasks of caring on their own. Sometimes this places an intolerable burden on them in terms of the restrictions it places on them, the limits on their choices in life and because it causes stress and ill health so that they are no longer able to cope and social services then become essential, and at a point where they are very expensive.

There are two further reasons why a person's social network should be the focus of attention in assessment and care management.

Social circumstances and individual characteristics

Firstly, a major thrust behind the community care reforms is the acknowledgment that the majority of people currently entering residential care do not want to be there and that many could have been maintained in their own homes with a relatively small amount of additional support from others (Neill et al, 1988; Shaw and Walton, 1979; Sinclair et al, 1990; Stapleton, 1976; Townsend, 1962; Willcocks et al, 1982). Residents are generally not more dependent on others for help with self care tasks than many people living in the community (Bebbington and Tong, 1986; Bowling and Bleatham, 1982; Booth et al, 1983; Neill et al, 1988; Wade et al, 1983). Housing, and particularly the retention of the person's own home, is a crucial factor in precipitating admissions and permanent placement (Neill et al, 1988; Townsend, 1962). Most residents were not receiving intensive packages of services that might have kept them at home (Avon, 1980; Neill et al, 1988), and as many as half of the applicants admitted from the community were not receiving home-help (Neill et al, 1988). In the opinion of social workers, between a third and a half of residents could have been kept at home given adequate support (Avon, 1980; Neill et al, 1988). **Most people enter residential care because of the relationships they have, or do not have, in their social circumstances and not just because of their individual characteristics.**

Supporting the carers

Secondly, researchers, and the developing carers' movement, have pointed out that to maintain people in their own homes, attention has to focus on the needs for support of carers, particularly close relatives, and the role played, or not played by people in the wider community (Bulmer, 1985; Levin et al, 1989; Parker, 1985; Power et al, 1983). This has been a major influence on community care reforms and specifically the aim "to ensure that providers make practical support for carers a high priority. Assessment of care needs should always take account of the needs of caring family, friends and neighbours." Enid Levin has pointed out that:

> "If this support is to be responsive to the individual, differing and changing needs of carers and their dependents, then it is essential that the providers of services have a clear understanding of: who cares for whom, why and in what circumstances; their experiences of caring and its consequences; and the kinds of services required." (Levin, 1991 p.1)

Responding to social relationships

Thus **social services and social work intervention are a response to the nature of a person's social relationships.** In many situations the relationship between the "client", their immediate "carer" and other support people, and how the situation can be maintained by supporting both, or all of these people, is of central concern.

The social situation as the unit of assessment

It follows that **the social situation is the appropriate unit of assessment.** It includes local and cultural expectations about "normal" patterns of care and support; the "clients'", the "carers'" and other significant people's perceptions of their needs and available resources; the judgments of other professionals; and the nature and quality of the care relationships that exist. All are an integral part of any future "package of care" which can be drawn from a combination of people's personal networks and the available voluntary and professional services.

Gathering people's perceptions

Each person in the social network of relatives, friends, neighbours and professionals such as the G.P., district nurse, occupational therapist, home care organiser, and so on, will have their own perception of "the problem", and opinion based on what they have been doing and could do to support the person at home. This information will be as crucial to "an assessment", as will be getting them all to work together to form the fluid set of human relationships that constitutes a "package of care".

**The assessment of the dependency needs of a person is insepar-
able from the dependability of others:** the people that exist in
the situation, the relatives, neighbours and other people in the
community who do, or could, provide some element of care and
support to the people traditionally seen as "clients", "service
users" and "carers".

Beyond Service Delivery

Conflicts of Interest and Social Control

How "problems" are defined

Not all social services work is directed at unmet need; much is focused on the **way** that needs are being met in the status quo. Social services and social workers are often involved because somebody has defined existing relationships as a problem, either because they are harmful to participants—some "mental health" and "child protection" referrals are obvious examples; or because a situation leads to unacceptable risks to a person concerned, e.g. some elderly people; or their behaviour causes risks to themselves or others, e.g. some mental illness referrals; or because a person's behaviour is defined as delinquent. All these situations involve several people: at least the "client" and the referrer, and typically many more, such as family, friends, neighbours and others including "victims" who, for many different reasons, share concern.

Implementing current policy

Assessment and care management is not just a straightforward matter of visiting someone, discussing their problems and needs, and arranging some services to meet those needs. The theoretical and research background which argues for this more complex vision of the realities of the task has been discussed in the previous sections. Here we focus on making more explicit some of the complexity of implementing current policy guidance, as a step towards subsequent identification of the strategic skills required by staff carrying out assessment and care management in a manner most likely to be empowering for those with whom they work.

Assessment, conflicting interests and empowerment

Where there are conflicts of interest and relationship or behaviour problems assessment will not be a single event in which the professional makes an "objective" judgment of the nature of the client's needs, which can then be met by the provision of a package of services organised by a provider. This report argues that an assessment is not just an event. Assessment is a **process** in which users and carers are or are not "empowered" to make informed choices and participate in the control of the arrangements that can be made for their care in the community. The Exchange model is a process through which people are: "given a greater individual say in how they live their lives and the services they need to help them to do so"; so that they are: "(able) to live as normal a life as possible in their own homes or in a homely environment in the local community"; and so that they are:

"provided with the right amount of care and support to help (them) achieve maximum possible independence and, by acquiring or re-acquiring basic living skills, helped to achieve their full potential." (*Caring for People* p.4; grammar amended.)

The studies of care management by Challis and colleagues reinforce the continuing nature of intervention:

"Neither the process of assessment nor of care packaging can be considered as a one-off activity. They are dynamic and build continuously on earlier work and require responses to changing circumstances and previously concealed problems". (Challis et al 1990, p.35).

Work Beyond Individuals

The worker as agent of change

The role of the professional social worker, assessor and/or care manager is not automatically that of direct care provider. It is normally **not** necessary for professionals to become an integral part of the process of meeting client needs. Instead their role can be that of an outsider, a broker who links those with needs to those who have the resources to meet them with or without purchasing services. Where intervention is required to modify people's behaviour, whether that of "clients" or of others whose decisions and actions lead to people's needs going unmet, workers will be required to act as agents of change (Smale et al, 1988).

Changes in professional attitudes

Griffiths followed Barclay in emphasising the crucial role of informal networks, spelling out a hierarchy of intervention beginning with the family and personal social networks, before professional services (Griffiths, 1988 p.1). It has been recognised that the implementation of these reforms requires a change in attitude, **from service-led provision with needs being identified for people, to consumer-led services with needs being defined by the people themselves.**

Changing the assumptions

But reliance on a change in attitude oversimplifies many of the situations that workers will be faced with when making assessments and putting together and managing packages of care. The "client" and the "consumer" are often assumed to be the same person and the natural target for social work and social services intervention. The emphasis placed on the needs of carers goes some way towards expanding the focus, but this in itself does not go far enough. To go further is to recognise that to change practice it is necessary to **change the assumptions that people make about the "individual" and "their problem" and "social problems".**

*"Individual" or
"social" problems?*

Many professionals and other people still see all problems in individual terms, and not in terms of all, or even some of the people who are part of the problem. We keep overlooking what it means to call them "social" services departments, acting as if they were really "individual" services departments; the enterprise "individual care at home" rather than "community" care (Whitaker, 1986; Smale, 1991). The reform of community care and child protection is in danger of being undermined by the basic assumptions that persist about the nature of the problems we are confronting.

*Expanding
individual choice*

An individual's choices are widened by presenting them with different options for their needs to be met, which means enabling them to choose between the different **people** who could meet those needs. Concentrating on them and "their needs", their internal or physical condition, does little or nothing to expand their choice. A move away from focusing on the individual towards the social network, or situation, will enhance not diminish the individual's options on "packages of care". Access to resources, buildings, transport and employment cannot be created by focusing on the individual needs of those currently denied opportunity, any more than care can be mobilised by concentrating on those who do not have it. If we are to maintain the integrity of "community" care, "social" service and "social" work, we have to confront the constant tendency that we all have to **regress to the individualisation of social problems.**

*What is a "social"
problem*

The discussion of what makes a problem a social problem is carried out in a review of research on community based management and practice and its implications for the reforms carried out in parallel with the production of this paper. In this it is argued that:

"People have many different problems, the causes located in many different aspects of their own attributes, their environment or in the interaction between the two. These 'causes' are not often known in a strictly scientific sense. These individual problems become a **social** problem when they are not resolved by the individual or when needs cannot be met by people in the immediate social circumstances of the person or people who 'have the problem'. Thus a frail, elderly woman having difficulty in feeding herself, fearful of being alone and without somebody with whom she can share her depression about her physical condition, clearly has 'problems'. Some may say these problems are an inevitable 'fact of life'; a feature of 'ageing'. For her to be referred to a social services or social work agency or in some other way to be identified as a **'social problem'** is more a comment on **how her problems are, or are not being met by others,** than on the condition itself. To focus on her and her needs alone is not only to ignore potential sources of support, in fact, the **normal** resources called on in these circumstances, it is to misunderstand the very nature of the **social problems** presented by this situation. When they do this, social service and other professionals stand little chance of producing positive change in the networks they have been called upon to help. They will depend on negotiating for state resources to help such people, and essentially take responsibility for these problems on to themselves as representatives of the state. This is a valid option and one which is vital for many. But it is far from the only option, and when used routinely it compounds the social services tendency to 'clientise' all who ask or are referred for help." (Smale et al, 1992)

Social problems are the malfunctioning of a network of people. The network may be composed of family, friends or neighbours, or other members of the wider community, or the "problem" may be that there are none, or too few, of these people. We have underlined the fact that the vast majority of people's needs are met by carers in the community, without professional intervention. People's needs only become a "social problem" when they are not met. Being old is not a serious problem any more than being a baby is one. Being either, without having appropriate relationships with others is, however, a "social problem". (Smale et al, 1988 pp. 122–3; Smale et al, 1992)

The Assessment of Need: Negotiation, the Care Management Team and "Packages of Care"

Knowing the options

Many people asking for help do not state their "needs" or "their problem", but ask for what they think is the right and/or their understanding of the only available solution. Typically they do not say "We need more support to help us look after our mother"; they say "She needs to go into residential care", because they think this is the only available option and they want or "need" social services to help them to execute this plan. Most people are ignorant of the options that could be available to them; indeed only a person who knows what the available services are can enter into a negotiation about matching needs to resources. There can be no real assessment of this situation without a full discussion of the alternatives. For most people a negotiation of the different perceptions of the problem and its possible solutions is an essential part of **assessment** and an integral part of the process of **care management**.

Community care and partnership

The reforms in "care in the community" do not have to be invented and are based on an awareness that services should be built on to the body of care that already exists in the community through partnerships with all concerned. This principle needs to be applied at the local level in developing alternative resources and at the individual level of a "package of care".

Developing alternative resources

It is possible to conceive of a situation of an isolated person where almost no caring relationships exists. But often even these people are referred by someone whose "care" is at least sufficient to contact social services for more help. This person has already acted on their monitoring of the situation, and supporting them to continue with this task may be an essential dimension of maintaining the person in their own home.

Let us return to Mrs Smith, Rose and Tom. It is inaccurate and unhelpful to see this as a referral to the social services to "put together" a package of care; one already exists. The significant issue is that a change in the situation, Mrs Smith's fall and admission to hospital, has caused other changes; changes to Rose and Tom's feelings about having her home, and this has in turn precipitated a referral to social services. It is possible that had the doctor or her colleagues managed the situation differently the referral would not have been made, just as it is possible that had more information about potential services been available the request might not have been made for residential care.

Negotiation and the Range of Work to be Done by the Care Management "Team"

All the components of social services work

The range and nature of the work to be undertaken by those carrying out assessments and care management can be illustrated by following the story of Mrs Smith, Rose and Tom further. A map of social services activities (Fig V), deduced from the management and practice of innovatory workers developing approaches to social work and social services delivery, based on partnerships with local people, recognises that social services work has the following components:

- work with individuals and their immediate families and network to tackle problems which directly affect them = **direct work**;

- work with wider community groups and other agencies to tackle problems which affect a range of people (including the individuals involved in direct work) = **indirect work**;

- work which involves the maintenance of certain social situations to avoid further distress or institutionalisation, by the provision of services = **service delivery**;

- work done to effect change in the ways people relate to each other, ways which precipitate or perpetuate social problems of family groups or at community levels = **change agent activities**.

It should be stressed that these dimensions are not alternatives. Somebody has to be doing something about all of them. They may be left to chance and the hope that they are available when needed, but not if the aim is to confront social problems rather than merely to rescue a few casualties, or have the resources to "put together packages of care".

Fig V: Map of Social Services Activities (*Smale et al, 1988*)

SERVICE DELIVERY

DIRECT WORK   WHO DOES WHAT WITH WHOM   INDIRECT WORK

WHO IS RESPONSIBLE FOR WHAT

CHANGE AGENT ACTIVITY

Putting together a "package of care"

Mrs Smith was referred for residential accommodation while in hospital following a fall. Rose and Tom feel they cannot have her home. An assessment is called for. This is **direct work** — not yet committed to change agent or service delivery work. The worker has been careful to explain that she is not necessarily there to offer help but to find out what people want and to see if anything can be organised. Rose and Tom have strongly conflicting feelings and need help in sorting out what they want and what they can realistically offer Mrs Smith. All three of them know very little about the alternatives available and nothing about their eligibility for benefits.

It is quickly ascertained that Rose and Tom feel unable rather than unwilling to cope with the demands of supporting Mrs Smith. Mrs Smith wants to get home as soon as possible. The worker recognises the need Rose and Tom express to have Mrs Smith out of Rose's way for part of the day. Mrs Smith, a gregarious woman, needs company. Tom does not want this to always be Rose.

The neighbourhood dimension and change

Now the worker uses the knowledge she has built up of the neighbourhood. She suggests that Rose and Tom contact the local carers' group. A colleague helped set this group up—but it is now self-sufficient but for small inputs of resources in the form of accommodation and administrative back-up.

The initiation of the group by the team member was **indirect change agent work**; the continuing maintenance functions, **indirect service delivery work**

The worker resumes **direct work** with Mrs Smith—now this is **change orientated;** the worker is not taking responsibility for the problem—she recognises that changes in views and in the pattern of relationships are needed if the care network is to be rebuilt, supported and extended.

She counsels Mrs Smith who is suffering the bereavement of lost physical capacity and independence and relives many of the experiences of the death of her partner. The worker also lays out the alternatives to Mrs Smith: residential care; or home, with certain conditions. Neither were originally Mrs Smith's choice but she, like most of us, cannot have everything.

A visit to a lunch club three days a week is suggested to further help Rose; Mrs Smith agrees to a trial period. The lunch club is run by a voluntary organisation financially supported by the social services department: **indirect service delivery**. It was established through a partnership between health visitors and social work department staff: more **indirect change agent activity and service delivery work.**

Negotiating who will do what?

The story could go on to describe the different interventions and arrangements that have to be made, as changes in any one person's contribution or circumstances has repercussions on the other people and services involved. Negotiation has to go on with all these people to ascertain who is doing what, who is prepared to do what under what circumstances. Mrs Smith, Rose and Tom have to be kept involved in, or at least abreast of all the discussions so that the agreements between all these people are reached. In this way a "package of care" is negotiated. The assessor or care manager will not know what the optimum package is before the other major parties do, because it cannot exist until all have agreed to do their part in receiving and giving support and services.

The package may include services bought by the care manager from private, voluntary or not-for-profit agencies. The care manager's work will continue as the situation is monitored and the various participants' perceptions of the situation and their capacity to contribute, change over time and to make sure that others renegotiate their part in the package, or to become directly involved in rearranging the part that people or service providers play. The work of those under formal contract will have to be monitored to ensure that services **are** delivered at the required standard for continued payments to be made.

The assessor and/or care manager have a vital part to play in identifying gaps where services need to be developed, in partnership with service users, those who could use help and other members of the local community, professionals in other agencies and team colleagues. Evidence drawn from the experience of care managers and their partners will be **the** vital building blocks of community care planning (Smale et al, 1992).

Supporting local initiative

The assessor and care manager's task will not be confined to services delivery. The very nature of the social problems which the care manager has to tackle, the complication represented by the social control and change agent tasks are not just minor preliminaries to the "real task" of providing services, nor are such activities confined to a small proportion of situations. There are many examples of area team and special project practice that synthesise the development of resources at this level with work with individuals and their carers (Bayley et al, 1989; Smale, 1991; Smale and Bennett, 1989). This is the work that Griffiths referred to when he said that the aim must be:

> "..to provide the structure and resources to support the initiative, the innovation and the commitment at the local level and to allow them to flourish." (Griffiths, 1988 p.iv)

The work of Challis and colleagues on care management provides further evidence for recognising the centrality of this dimension of the task. In their study of the nature of the problems dealt with by care managers, they write:

> "Not uncommonly, the package of care consisted of mobilising and reorganising the input of existing services . . . this often required patient, tactful negotiations . . . Neighbours, family and friends sometimes preferred not to commit themselves to undertaking certain activities at particular times of the day . . . Fine judgments were required about when and how it was necessary to intervene in family support to improve the quality of care without interfering unreasonably in the lives and relationships of others . . ."
> (Challis et al, 1990 p.32)

The complexities of care management

Assessment and care management will often include attempts to bring about changes in the behaviour of people in the network, since what is being "provided" is resource from inside the existing network obtained through interventions by the "purchaser". For example, in the situation of the Smith family, the care manager enters into several negotiations, with Mrs. Smith, Rose and Tom, with all three as a group, with colleagues and other professionals, etc. Such negotiations **are** the process of care management, through which certain changes occur. A part of the negotiation with Mrs. Smith about how to get her dependency needs met, includes what might conventionally be described as "bereavement counselling". This emerges as a necessary part of the process of negotiation, and is not just a separately provided service, although it could be if further help with particularly complex problems was required. Mrs. Smith shifts some of her expectations. It becomes possible for her to consider attendance at a lunch club, which is one of the changes necessary to support Tom and Rose to continue caring for Mrs. Smith. These are only a small part of the total set of changes which the people who are part of Mrs Smith's network will be involved in, and which the care manager will have to facilitate. Such processes of change within a pattern of relationships are an essential part of empowering users and carers in the ways they manage their problems of living, and particularly, their dependency needs.

Resolving relationship problems

Challis et al write:
"On some occasions it was necessary to deal with considerable conflict in an informal care network, arising from misperceptions between elderly person and carer, and attempting to resolve problems of hidden stress, guilt and difficulties in relationships. On other occasions work involved shifting the balance of demands within family groups to avoid polarisation of care on one individual." (Challis et al, 1990 p.47)

Of this kind of negotiation and conflict management process they write:
"Indeed, work supporting families and dealing with conflicts in relationships was identified as the most important problem across the reviews, and therefore of the care manager's workload" (Challis et al, 1990 p.40)

Putting Together "Packages of Care" and the Availability of Human and Other Resources

The full implementation of the NHS and Community Care and the Children Acts will give social services departments greater power to buy services from other providers and much emphasis has been given to this dimension of the reforms.

The availability of services

Just as the bulk of care in the community is provided by ordinary citizens, so it is that many of the additions and alternatives come from community-based resources and not directly from professional workers. It is neither desirable that these should be replaced by professional services, whether private or public, nor is it likely that the finance to do so could be made available. It is also not certain that such a switch would empower more people; there is no clear automatic reason why people should be less patronised by private welfare provision than they are by public services.

Building on local resources

The stated intention of the Griffiths report was to set up the machinery to put the recommendations of the Barclay report into practice (Griffiths, 1988 p.197). It is essential that we do not overlook the principle of building on the resources that exist at the local level to expand the range of available resources. We have seen how vital these services were for Mrs Smith, Rose and Tom.

There is a considerable body of experience to be drawn on from research and development work on building on the so called "informal sector", "interweaving formal and informal care" and the development of support in social networks. (Bayley et al, 1985; Hadley and McGrath, 1984; Smale and Bennett, 1989; Darvill and Smale, 1990). Critics have drawn attention to the limitations of the care available in social networks, and the need to deliberately set out to develop such capacity rather than leave them to chance (Bulmer, 1987; Finch and Groves, 1983; Smale et al, 1988).

Challis and his colleagues have also drawn attention to the need for care managers to work beyond the level of individual cases and to engage in developing local resources (Challis and Davies, 1986; Challis et al, 1990). The literature of the Community Social Work Exchange contains many examples of such development work and the steps that teams need to go through to expand access to resources in partnership with local people (Smale and Bennett, 1989; Darvill and Smale, 1990; Smale et al, 1988). The NISW research on innovatory schemes studied the organisational characteristics that promote or inhibit such work and a subsequent guide helps agencies to develop these aspects of their practice (Crosbie and Vickery, 1989; Miller, Crosbie and Vickery, 1991). A review of the implications of this and related research and development literature for the implementation of the reforms has been prepared in conjunction with this report (Smale et al, 1992).

Expanding the care options

Research has differentiated between the kinds of care that are acceptable to those in need and provided by close personal relatives or professionals, for example bathing, and the support that is offered by neighbours and other members of the community, for example occasional shopping (Sinclair et al, 1988). NISW's Networks Research Project for example, found that many elderly people wanted personal care to be carried out by a paid person if no close relative was available. This differing evidence reflects the many different variables that exist in disparate neighbourhoods and cultures. Development work undertaken with practitioners and managers from around the country has underlined the differences that exist from community to community and the need to develop services accordingly (Smale et al, 1988). It has also emphasised the need for managers to organise their staff, and specifically the workload, to develop the resources required to expand the available options of care in the community. But the same development work has also indicated that resources can be developed if teams of social services staff adopt a broad range of activities (Smale et al, 1992).

Empowerment and the Management of Local Resources

Working with local people

This report focuses on the interface between professionals and citizens as they work together to arrive at assessments of the latter's needs and the management of their care. However partnerships need to be formed for service users to be involved in the planning of services. The care manager and her immediate colleagues will be involved in indirect work as well as direct service provision and change agent work with people. During the process of carrying out an assessment with Mrs Smith, Rose and Tom, the worker has drawn on:

- a local carers' group that a colleague helped set up. Other colleagues in the department provide resources in the form of accommodation and administrative back-up.

- a lunch club run by a voluntary organisation, financially supported by the social services department, and established through a partnership between health visitors and social work department staff.

Care managers will have to work in partnership with local people to negotiate the need for, plan, initiate, support, sustain and maintain local groups, voluntary organisations and schemes for meeting certain people's needs. People like Rose, Tom and Nellie often become important members of the management of such projects as well as their beneficiaries. The skills that we identify in Part Two have been identified with this level of partnership in mind.

Categories of partnership

Miller, Crosbie and Vickery identified four main categories of partnerships that workers in social services departments will have with such schemes:

- **working with community groups**—where the social services department enables an existing or new community group to set up and continue to run its own community care scheme;

- **working with secondary volunteers**—where the area office collaborates with an organisation like a local church because it has access to its own volunteers;

- **working with existing voluntary organisations**—where the social services department collaborates with other statutory, voluntary or private agencies to run community care schemes;

- **setting up and working with newly formed voluntary organisations with paid staff**—where the area office is instrumental in setting up a new voluntary organisation which has its own staff." (Miller, Crosbie and Vickery, 1991)

User participation

Croft and Beresford's (1990) study of schemes that have pioneered user participation suggest that there are two crucial components that workers should strive to guarantee:

> "The schemes that were studied suggest that a two-fold approach is essential if involvement is to be representative and a positive experience for would-be participants. The crucial components are **support** and **access**. People need to be offered personal support and skills to take part, combined with suitable structures and opportunities for involvement in social services agencies.

> Unless both are present people may either lack the confidence, expectations or abilities to get involved, or be discouraged by the difficulties entailed. Without them, participatory initiatives are likely to **reinforce** rather than overcome existing race, class, gender and other inequalities." (Croft and Beresford, 1990)

Teamwork in Assessment and Care Management

Teams of people, not "packages of care"

In the review of research and development work on community based practice the authors wrote:

> **"A package of care is not like a basket of goods and services: it is actually a fluid set of human relationships and arrangements.** The care manager's main task will be to make the efforts of the people involved coherent; to make sure that the care of a dependent person is not dropped like the baton of a badly co-ordinated relay team. **Teamwork between these people is essential and the care manager's role will focus on team development and maintenance."** (Smale et al, 1992)

The image of a "package" can be very misleading. This may be appropriate to describe some components such as aids and adaptations, finance and buildings but neither the care parents provide for their children nor that provided for other dependent people can be conceived of as a "package" in this limited sense.

What a particular person wants, who they expect to meet their different needs, what they and their carers expect and want from services has to be discovered and negotiated by workers in each case. Tailor-made solutions have to become the norm. At best, off the peg solutions fit by chance; at worst, they cause grave offence and cause minority groups to be deprived of services altogether.

Empowerment and the reinvention of practice

In the Introduction we said:

> "To empower the particular people they work with and respond to the unique circumstances that confront them on a day by day basis, professionals have to **reinvent** their practice

and their perception of particular problems and solutions in each different social situation that they find themselves in."

Specialists within local teams

The range of tasks represented by the map (Fig V) is potentially very wide, often more than the whole range of social service activities currently found in all but the most innovatory community-based teams. Within the agency there will have to be a high degree of collaboration between the workers engaged in providing a coherent service through a division of labour. In the companion review we draw attention to the research implications that indicate that this is best achieved by locating specialists within geographically located generalist teams, who can maintain as intimate a set of relationships with the local community as possible.

Devolved decision making

Responsibility for essential decisions should be located with those people who actually know most about the situation (Smale et al, 1991; Sinclair et al, 1990). The home care organiser, or more likely the home-help, not only may know most about services, but much more significantly, will know most about the needs, the situation of the client and carers and changes in these circumstances. This level of staff should be major contributors to decision-making in the process of assessment and care management since relative to others in the professional network, they are likely to be best informed. It is crucial to avoid a split between those who are in day-to-day or frequent contact, and those who make decisions about what is to be done and the allocation of resources. Splitting these two will inevitably be disempowering to the users and carers since they are the people who know most about their situation.

Teamwork between ALL participants

Teamwork across agency and professional boundaries is also essential to achieve the collaboration advocated by Griffiths, *Caring for People* and the implementation guidelines. It is above all essential at the "street level" between the team members who are the people in a package of care.

If people's needs are not to be dropped between the actions of all those involved, those who make up a package of care will have to be coordinated in such a way that, as in the metaphorical relay race, the changeovers are smooth and the care is consistent, if not actually required to be as continuous. Many adults are "care managers" for a significant part of their lives. The "care management" of working mothers, and increasingly working fathers, is a good example of the constant juggling that is required to make sure that their children's need for care and protection are covered twenty-four hours a day. All of us who have participated in this process, whether for children or adults with care needs, know that flexibility is a crucial dimension and that the best planned systems can be thrown by a person's temporary absence and havoc caused by chronic or random inconsistency. People who care because of family or other "moral" obligations are constantly expected to "do a little bit extra" at the cost of their choice, and "empowerment". Whoever the service provider is, there is no room in a "package of care" for a "demarcation dispute" leading to a "work to rule" or people "walking off the job" regardless before the end of a shift. A crucial dimension of the care manager's function is to sustain this teamwork over time just as the assessor's task is to work with potential participants and recipients to negotiate the optimum set of arrangements. Remember, in most situations there is no professional care manager. Where there will be one, they will often be supplementary to the person normally managing and providing care for the dependent person, or people. Partnership and teamwork between the people are essential.

Rethinking social work and social services

The skills required to participate in practice through teamwork at all levels are reviewed in Part Two. Elsewhere we have argued that the development of these skills requires a radical rethinking of the nature and location of social work and social services staff development, education and training (Smale and Tuson, 1988).

We have stressed that an empowering approach to assessment and care management has to recognise that assessment involves an understanding of a social situation, of the pattern of relationships in which a person's needs are perceived by somebody as not being met. It is not just the assessment of an individual but of the relationship between them and the people with the resources to support or to change the situation.

Social policy and social care planning adopts a wide-angle lens perspective, taking in the whole of the community. The orthodox approach to social work practice and community care has been to view problems through a telephoto lens, seeing the individual in clear focus; the surrounding environment is either hazy or ignored. The "unitary" and "integrated methods" approaches to practice suggested adopting a zoom lens approach, enabling us to rapidly switch focus from the individual to community, first intervening at one level and next, or at the same time, working for change at other levels. It is necessary to go beyond these ways of looking at problems, to recognise that the relationships that make up care in the community are all around the viewer and that the observer is an integral part of the action. With this approach the care manager is an integral part of the package of care, requiring the worker to participate and monitor the consequences of their own actions and those of others as they unfold in the flux of change over time.

This is not an unnecessary complication but a necessary recognition of the complexity of people's lives, which are normally managed by members of the public who manage the care of their children with that of their dependent relatives and neighbours.

From Assessment into Care Management

Care management and assessment have to be viewed as aspects of the same process, and the care manager will always at some level have to be centrally involved in assessment, monitoring and reviewing outcomes. As in the example of Mrs Smith, in practice the two will be mixed over time.

The care manager is responsible for helping networks of people solve or ameliorate their joint problem. This includes members of the care manager's own organisation as a significant part of the client's network and hence by definition a part of the problem. The care manager has to take responsibility for assessment of all those dimensions. She can negotiate some division of the task, and ensure that other people carry out their own assessment responsibilities, but she must retain responsibility for the management of this network of information. Consequently, the care manager requires all the knowledge and skills necessary for assessing and bringing about change in complex social networks, whether she is doing this directly herself, or indirectly through delegation, since either way it will involve working with networks. The care manager will maintain a changing assessment, and remain involved with the networks of people concerned, at some level, in order to participate in the inevitable renegotiations and reassessments that will have to occur as circumstances change over time. The care manager will need to recognise that they do not manage those processes alone; that service users and carers should often be major decision makers and often control more, so-called informal, resources.

PART TWO

The Skills of Assessment and Care Management

The main tasks

In this discussion assessment and care management are assumed to be a continuous process carried out by a single person, or by people within the same team, and in partnership with several others. As already argued, the main tasks are to:

- facilitate full participation in the processes of decision making;

- make a "holistic" assessment of the social situation, and not just of the referred individual;

- help create and maintain the flexible set of human relationships which make up a "package of care";

- facilitate negotiations within personal networks about conflicts of choice and needs;

- create sufficient trust for full participation and open negotiations to actually take place;

- change the approach to all these broad tasks as the situation itself changes over time.

Interpersonal skills

The care manager needs the knowledge and skills necessary to manage, or lead, the processes of negotiation with others which essentially constitute assessment, and the management of a "package of care". These are interpersonal skills because the task centrally requires the care manager to work with and help co-ordinate the knowledge, skills and personal time of the people involved in specific instances of community care. To do this they will use their own behaviour and knowledge to facilitate all necessary negotiations and monitor the performance of formal and informal contracts. Holding and using a budget, gatekeeping goods and service, counselling individuals, are not ends in themselves. They are tools for helping people work together differently in tackling the social problems which they experience or attempt to help with.

People who carry out "care management" functions because they are family members, friends or neighbours use the relationship and organisational skills that they have to contribute to, and organise, care for their dependents. Professionals are expected to be able to consistently apply such skills to working with a wide cross-section of people in the different communities that make up our society. It is also expected that they are committed to developing their repertoire so that they will be able to relate to people from different ethnic groups beyond their own personal experience or to form partnerships with people who can. The professional should also bring a knowledge of the services available to meet the needs of people in the community and have collaborative relationships with other professionals, agencies and community resources to be able to present choices to those in need and negotiate with all concerned to agree who should do what with whom.

Working within the community

The professional will also be part of an agency team engaged in planning services for people in a particular community, be that determined by geography or membership of a particular social group. We have stressed in Part One that this responsibility will take work beyond the circumstances of the individual and work with community groups and other agencies to expand the resources available to people, and so increase choices. This includes effective communication with a wide range of people.

A high order of skill is required of a care manager to have such a communication repertoire and to consistently carry out these strategic tasks.

Mapping the essential skills

There are indications from a wide and diverse range of literature about the interpersonal skills required for these kinds of activities. These include outcome research into the behaviour of professionals in a wide range of "helping" relationships and "user studies" that have looked at the experience of those receiving professional help. Two extracts from reviews of user studies will highlight what users appreciate and guide our mapping of essential skills.

Enid Levin, in reviewing research relevant to *Carers—Problems, Strains and Services*, underlines the importance of the second key objective of *Caring for People* (DoH, 1989): "to ensure that service providers make practical support for carers a high priority". She writes:

> "If this support is to be responsive to the individual, differing and changing needs of carers and their dependents, then it is essential that the providers of services have a clear understanding of: who cares for whom, why and in what circumstances; their experiences of caring and its consequences; and the kinds of services required." (Levin, 1991 p.1)

What people value from professionals

The DHSS summary of research on child care decision-making succinctly portrays what people valued from professionals who provide services, intervene and participate in major decisions that affect their lives:

> "All the research projects which included interviews with parents reported similar messages from them. What was appreciated most was honesty, naturalness and reliability,

along with an ability to listen. Clients appreciated being kept informed, having their feelings understood, having the stress of parenthood accepted and getting practical help as well as moral support. The social workers whose assistance was valued had a capacity to help parents retain their role as responsible authority figures in relation to their children. These workers were actively involved in the processes, negotiations and family dynamics of admissions and discharge. When these qualities were present, social work help was highly valued". (DHSS, 1985 p.20)

Theory and research which supports and gives operational meaning to such commonsense notions as "honesty" and the "ability to listen" forms the basis of our understanding of the skills required by staff undertaking care management and assessment, and which are mapped out and discussed below.

Joining with People: The First Steps

A major prerequisite for the care manager to be able to carry out the tasks described is the ability to join with people; the ability to create a collaborative working relationship wherever necessary. Three of the central skills required for this are now discussed.

Authenticity: The care manager's ability to relate to others with integrity; to be aware of their own feelings and values as well as the significance of their agency role and the other roles they occupy dependent upon gender, race and cultural background.

A capacity for authenticity, or congruence, has to inform all the actions and communications of the care manager. There are several levels to this, from the straightforward demand that workers are honest with people about themselves, their agencies and resources, to the more sophisticated demands on the worker's self-awareness and use of self in facilitating complex processes of change.

The evidence

Authenticity is identified as an important quality and set of behaviours in a wide and diverse literature including: counselling and interpersonal helping research (Macdevitt, 1987; Egan, 1990; Patterson, 1984); family therapy and group work literature (Gurman and Kniskern, 1978; Minuchin, 1981; Smale, 1983; Smith, Wood and Smale, 1980); the literature on Black perspectives in social work (Ahmad B., 1990); research in child care (DHSS, 1985; Fisher et al, 1986) ; current research into the use of task-centred approaches (Biehal, 1991); and some of the literature on community care (Darvill and Smale, 1990; Smale and Bennett, 1989). Some of these are discussed in more detail below.

Beyond the bureaucratic role

If those carrying out assessments and subsequent care management are to relate to their fellow citizens as "partners" rather than as "clients" then it is important that care managers do not fall into the trap of "role-playing" their part in the relationship. It is essential that workers do not approach these relationships as a faceless representative of their agency but as a genuine human being, a fellow citizen willing to share in tackling a problem with others. Professionals will of course represent their agencies. This representation should not govern their behaviour but be a natural part of the baggage that they bring with them to relationships; hopefully they have in it knowledge of services and potential solutions that the other people in the situation may not have, and they are the keys to resources that they and their agency are responsible for distributing or gatekeeping.

To enter negotiations as an equal citizen it is crucial that the care manager be open and straightforward, and go beyond playing a bureaucratic role. Equally it is unhelpful, dishonest, and ultimately disempowering merely to simulate understanding of the situation or person, or pretend to a level of interest or care which is not actually experienced. Such phoney communication is generally noticed, and if not overtly commented on by the other person, will nevertheless affect their judgment of the worker, and their behaviour in response.

It is a part of the communication of respect for the user, carer and others involved that the care manager is "straight" in all the communications which constitute the work.

Being open with people

When the worker involved with the Smiths makes her initial contact she is not immediately committed to either service delivery work or change agent work. It was said above that "the worker has been careful to explain that she is not necessarily there to help but to find out what people want and to see if anything can be organised". The worker, being open with people about her position, and being sufficiently self-aware to realise the importance of being open about this, is an example of worker's authenticity. She does not pretend to know what to do, or unrealistically imply that a solution is actually available before she has negotiated some shared understanding of the issues.

Building bridges

A major part of the care manager's task is to build bridges between people, create and maintain links, and help negotiations and re-negotiations. The professional worker has to join with the dependent people, the carers that already exist and those who potentially exist in the social situation and in the wider community, and people in other agencies. This requires the worker simultaneously to be actor, participant and observer in often complex social situations and there is a continual risk of the worker being knocked off track by all the different, and often conflicting, pressures. As a consequence, it is crucial the care manager remains aware of his or her own feelings, perceptions, values and the impact of their gender, race and cultural background on the people they are relating to.

The skills required

The Personal Social Services Research Unit (PSSRU) study of the Gateshead scheme identified skills which assume worker authenticity. For example: "Engagement: form effective relationship with client and family . . . Provide continued emotional support and counselling where appropriate . . ." (Challis et al, 1990 p.9)

If these skills were "unpacked" the skill of authenticity would become more explicit—for example, an "effective relationship" will be one characterised by congruent communications etc., and this is true for all the other skills listed in this literature.

The discussion in the SWIP research on "routinised responses" and "problem identification" is relevant here. For example, "routine assessments" for residential care were:

> ". . . sometimes approached as if they were primarily an administrative task, simply a question of filling in forms. Unlike the admission of children to residential care this transition was not always viewed by professionals as a major life event which could be very stressful for the individual involved". (Biehal, 1991 p.2)

Actual behaviour and espoused values

The issue of congruence here is that it is likely that the workers involved would claim knowledge of theories of loss, for example, and maybe claim some empathy for the client's experience, but actually behave in contrary, that is incongruent, ways. Also such "administrative" behaviour is very likely to be inconsistent with the espoused values of the organisation for which they work. A major and widespread issue is the failure of staff at all levels to "practice what they preach", and to do otherwise is to behave inauthentically.

Working with minority ethnic groups

The issue of authenticity is a major one for writers on work with minority ethnic groups. Bandana Ahmad writes:

> "Feeling warmth, concern, empathy etc. are nothing new in social work practice. Acquisition and application of these skills are fundamental to the social work encounter. However, the social work encounter with Black clients often has difficulties in applying these fundamental skills. These difficulties may vary from personal prejudice against Black people in general to dislike or disapproval of the behaviour or values of Black people—or simple paranoia and mental block in dealing with Black clients. It is imperative that these difficulties are acknowledged by social workers." (Ahmad B., 1990 p.34)

Staff may have to make a range of personal changes in their attitudes and behaviours in relation to Black people in order for them to be able to work congruently with them.

"Person to person" relations

We are reminded of Carkhuff's advice to counsellors. He recognised that professionals and their clients inevitably come together in different roles but asserted that an aim of the worker should be to "work through roles to relate to the other 'person to person'." (Carkhuff, 1971).

Empathy: Empathy is used here to refer to a person's ability to communicate understanding; to understand what the other person is thinking and feeling, their position, their perception of the situation and what they want.

This definition of empathy does not refer to an intuitive understanding of another person or people, or to some near telepathic power, nor does it mean a "natural sympathy" for a person or other people. It is not even enough to understand a person and be able to communicate this to a third person. Although all of these dimensions may go with an empathic understanding of another person, they are not sufficient.

The complex process of communication

Empathy refers to the hard work of hearing, comprehending and communicating understanding of what other people say, the thoughts and feelings that they express and the way that they make sense of the world. The worker builds up such understanding by checking that they have heard what the other person meant to say, so that there is a convergence of their perceptions of the situation, the problems that have to be resolved, the potential resources available and possible solutions. The acknowledgment of empathy as a technical skill to be constantly developed recognises that communication is a complex process as different people inevitably start from different backgrounds and assumptions and even if they use the same language, words will have different meanings. Obviously communication between people from different ethnic, cultural and class backgrounds presents particular difficulties and will require specific attention. As with any language skills, the naturalness of empathy develops over time and with practice but has to be relearnt on entering a new culture. The test of empathy between people is that people know that they are understood because they know and agree with the other person's understanding of them.

Hearing what people say

Rose and Tom, it is said, "feel unable, rather than unwilling to cope with Mrs. Smith". The worker "recognises the need Rose and Tom express to have Mrs. Smith out of Rose's way for part of the day". It would be quite easy and natural to misinterpret Rose and Tom's initial view that they cannot have Mrs. Smith home from hospital as unwillingness, rather than an expression of their view of their inability. It is crucial that the worker has the ability to encourage them to explore their own feelings and perceptions sufficiently to get this distinction explicit. To do that requires the worker to engage in the difficult work of really hearing what people are saying and checking on her understanding.

The evidence

The collaborative inter-personal, problem-solving task central to care management and assessment requires that the care manager has some minimal ability to understand the experience of all the people in the network with whom he or she is having to work, and to successfully communicate that understanding to them. A wide range of literature reinforces this (Egan, 1990; Raines, 1990; Barkham, 1988; Smale 1983, 1987; Roger, 1986; Elliott, 1985; Wodarski and Bagarozzi, 1979).

Specific recent work on community care reinforces this wider literature. For example Challis and colleagues write:
>   "Entree refers to the difficulty of gaining access to and acceptance by the elderly person: first for the social worker and later

for the care or help which they wished to provide. This could mean at first gaining an understanding of the old person's routine, which at times required considerable persistence and 'detective work' as a means of identifying ways of establishing rapport and communication". (Challis et al, 1990 p.98)

The establishment of rapport, which includes demonstrating understanding of the person's "routine" or current way of life, is another, (though less precise) way of talking about the need for "empathy" in the sense defined.

In the Gateshead study Challis and colleagues (1990) write:
"The way in which help was offered in the approach of both the case manager and the helpers appeared to be crucial to effective outcomes. Often a pattern of one-to-one communication had to be resurrected as elderly people had often been talked over on the assumption that they were unable to understand". (p.45)

Empathy and empowerment

Empathic understanding as defined above is "empowering" in one major way. To empathise is often to assume that the other person is the "expert" in their problem and their situation, and that the task is to help them develop their own understanding in ways that encourage remaining in control of their goals and options. Many other behaviours that a care manager might naturally use in the process of assessment and care management will tend to "disempower" in comparison. For example, questioning and probing without prior establishment of rapport may be experienced as carrying many implicit assumptions about the situation: patronising interpretation of the "real meaning" of what someone has communicated; simply not listening effectively; systematically misunderstanding; telling people what to do; ignoring them, etc.

Taking empathy for granted

It is often taken for granted that professional staff are skilled at empathising, either because it is assumed that they are selected as naturally empathic people or that they develop these skills through basic professional education or training. However this probably cannot be safely assumed to be the case (Smale, 1983; 1987).

The limitations of an interrogative approach

Recent controversy about the interviewing of children believed to have been sexually abused points up the dangers of "questioning". For example, a series of court judgments reported in *Family Law Review* (1987, pp.269–343) which involved detailed examination of the interactions between professional staff and children allegedly the victims of sexual abuse, clearly demonstrate the limitations of a "questioning" or interrogative approach to the facilitation of communication. In these reports the value of the data generated by questioning is challenged on the grounds that it is not evidentially sound, with the implication that it may yet be "clinically" acceptable. However, this seems a distinction of doubtful value, since presumably the clinician, or come to that the care manager, no more wants information aimed merely at satisfying the questioner than does the judge or jury. The care manager, like any professional trying to assess a social situation and work out in partnership with others what to do, needs to hear what people's actual concerns and preoccupations are. They do not need to hear merely what the person thinks they want to hear, as deduced from the questions to which they are subjected—they need to hear the other person's honest perceptions, expressed in their own language, and at their own pace, and which the worker may have to work hard at understanding. The difficulties of actually achieving this level of mutual understanding, and convergence of perceptions, cannot be short-circuited by "questioning" even under the pressure from other people to do something quickly, as happens in situations of child sexual abuse, but equally often in situations involving the care of the elderly, for example. The requirement for information uncontaminated by the professionals' expectations and interpretations is as vital for the clinician, policeman, and judge, as it is for the care manager, and the dangers of this requirement not being met are as great.

Confrontation and racism

It is a central theme of much of the literature on work with minority ethnic groups that their experience is not listened to, and if listened to, not heard or understood; and this includes not "hearing" the capacity of Black people to understand and empathise with white people, including professional staff. For example, Bandana Ahmad, in discussing how social workers can develop their skills of confrontation without being racist argues that:

> "An essential requisite of an ongoing programme of self-evaluation is self-confrontation, i.e. confronting one's own approach and incentive for expressing warmth, concern and empathy that may be insensitive to the Black client's dignity and pride (e.g. patronising), or may not relate to the real problems of the Black client (e.g. concentrating on those aspects of the problem that least require expression of warmth, concern and empathy)". (Ahmad B., 1990 p.35)

"Starting where the client is at"

The need for skilled empathic understanding by the care manager is particularly crucial in work with minority ethnic groups because of the special risk of phoney, and thus patronising and irrelevant, understanding. This risk is also a general one. For example, the SWIP research re-identifies the old wisdom of "starting where the client is at".

In order to enter into meaningful negotiations with all the people in the network, it is necessary to start with, that is, hear, empathise with and accept, each person's initial perceptions of the problem. Some of these may have to be challenged, but this will not be successful unless those people experience the care manager at least communicating understanding of, that is empathising with, their starting point. For example, Nina Biehal writes:

"In focusing initially on problems prioritised by the client the worker may be able to gain the elderly person's trust and demonstrate their commitment to giving the client a genuine degree of control over the work undertaken. It may then be possible to negotiate with the client a commitment to working on additional problems . . . In one case studied by SWIP, for example, a worker commented that it had been impossible to engage the client in working on any of her other problems until she had helped her resolve the financial difficulties that were troubling her." (Biehal, 1991 p.3).

Tracking not leading

We have stressed that empathy involves tracking and not leading the person's description of their situation with questions based on the professional's agenda. We would underline the principles identified in the DoH publication *Getting the Message Across*. The authors point out that an assessment should "strike a balance between invading privacy and obtaining sufficient information to gain an understanding of need". To empower and assess it is necessary to recognise that the worker arrives at this understanding with the other people assessed and not ahead of them. The gatekeeper of privacy should always be the person who has the relevant "secrets". They will reveal them when they decide they are relevant and that the recipient is trustworthy. This leads us on to consider the significance of "respect".

Respect: The care manager's ability to communicate their acceptance and valuation of people irrespective of their personal qualities and social or professional position.

The entire movement towards greater service user and carer involvement in the planning and design of community care can be understood as an attempt to operationalise an underlying value of respect. How this is carried through at "street-level" by the care manager in the process of assessment and the development of "packages of care", is therefore crucial. Respect in this sense is shown in the general orientation of the care manager toward the user, carer, and other people involved in the care network. Respect is shown in the consistency and quality of empathy and authenticity; it is shown by the worker seriously thinking about, or conceptualising the uniqueness of the situation and the people involved and avoiding stereotyped responses; it is shown by a willingness and ability to challenge people to use their strengths and risk change.

Respect is shown in the worker's recognition that they themselves are but ordinary citizens attempting to apply their particular knowledge and skills to sort out a social situation to arrange for some of the needs of some of the people to be met. Another way of putting this is to say that the worker recognises that all the people in the situation have expert knowledge of the situation and resources to draw on to contribute to a package of care that will maintain the situation.

The PSSRU studies, in a discussion of responding to elderly people with "intellectual impairment", provide considerable evidence of the central need for the care manager to be able to communicate respect, in the sense outlined, in many different ways. For example:

> ". . . the aim was to re-establish life patterns rather than impose an unfamiliar external routine which is often inevitable using existing services. This required the care manager to identify what skills remained, and what was meaningful to the elderly person and to build on that identified routine." (Challis et al, 1990 p.46)

Respecting the life patterns of the client by taking the trouble to identify them, validating them and helping the client build on them, are all dimensions of the capacity to communicate respect. One of the child care team leaders in the SWIP research summed it up in a follow-up interview in a very similar way:

> ". . . after the training it's possible now to stand up more and say 'this job I'm doing should be all about treating people with respect'; in fact it makes it more easy to approach people on that sort of level" (SWIP, 1991).

This idea of "respect" has been discussed in many research and theoretical traditions relevant to assessment and care management. It has long been considered a core value of social work, and has been given practical definition, for example in the work of Egan (1990); Harre (1980); Norcross, Stausser and Faltus (1988). Two decades of task-centred research in social work also provide detailed material as to how a user orientation, a collaborative relationship and a focus on problem-solving process can be applied (Fortune, 1985; Reid, 1992, 1987 and 1988; Doel and Marsh, 1992).

The capacity to communicate respect is not restricted to the individual level. The communication of respect also includes and involves respect for collective viewpoints, and group resources. This is especially highlighted by Black perspectives on social work and care in the community. For example, Arshi Ahmad writes:

> "Black people and therefore Black communities are too frequently perceived as having needs and not strengths . . . The exercise of social control by Black communities must be supported and strengthened, and not undermined by either the department's procedures or individual worker's practice." (Ahmad A., 1990 p. 26)

The SWIP researchers support the importance of this dimension of the care manager's skills when they describe, for example, the danger of the worker who:

> ". . . does not engage with the elderly person as a partner capable of autonomous decisions about which degree of independent action they might choose to take . . . but instead unilaterally decides on their behalf what degree of autonomy they should be capable of." (SWIP, 1991 p.5)

Putting it all Together: Patterning and Arranging

The three core skills just discussed can be seen as those central to the strategic care management task of **joining** with the different individuals who make up the social situation under review and the overlapping networks of people who may constitute the current or potential "package of care". Beyond such "joining", the care manager will need to bring all the components together: to negotiate who can, and will do what to support whom. For this the care manager will need to be competent in the four areas now discussed.

Marginality: The worker's ability to operate effectively as a participant and as an observer in any circumstance, and to neither become a part of problem-perpetuating interactions, slip unintentionally into being a permanent part of "the solution", nor remain impotently on the outside of the networks of people with whom they are involved.

Developing a neutral perspective

It has been argued above that social problems need to be understood as the malfunctioning of a network. Consequently, care managers are never relating just to individuals: they are always relating to overt and covert networks of people, and consciously attempting to maintain or change the patterns of relationships. Often members of that network are not asking the care manager to help them as individuals to change, as they would if approaching a counsellor. More often, it is a relative, or a neighbour, or someone from another agency, trying to get the care manager to "do something" about the dependent person or support the carer. This "referrer" may, of course, be seen by the care manager as part of the problem, and hence as a target for change. In order to facilitate the negotiations which will be necessary between different members of this network, it is essential that someone, most obviously the care manager, be able to develop a relatively neutral "outside" perspective to the network.

It is important that the worker can exercise the skills that have been outlined above to "join" with people but retain an impartiality, a neutrality based on their lack of vested interest and ability to see the point of view of all the parties in the situation. This impartiality is at the heart of the purchaser-provider split. To split these functions is easy when thinking of buying and providing services (in conceptual terms, at least). However, it is more complex when the currency is not money, and the transaction is the communication of different people's perceptions of their needs, their feelings and their choices over how their care, that is their set of crucial relationships, is to be organised and maintained. The ability of the worker to understand, to empathise without getting sucked into the swamp of feelings and vested interests and so perform the functions of the honest broker, is what we mean by marginality. Someone needs to have this order of overview in order to help the people involved decide who should do what next, and to help them re-negotiate the division of labour if necessary, especially where there are conflicts of interest and perceptions.

The "honest broker"

The worker involved with the Smith family has to be able to join with the people sufficiently to hear Mrs. Smith's sadness and loss and her desire to return home; Rose's feelings of being trapped by the responsibility, but also guilt at seeming to reject her mother; Tom's protectiveness towards Rose and his own legitimate interests; and so forth. However, she cannot simply "take sides" in this situation, and promote a particular interest in the conflict. This will be difficult since the people will, quite naturally, tend to provoke different responses in the worker, and overtly or covertly promote certain alliances. The worker somehow has to maintain what we have described as a marginal position. This is dynamic, and has to change as the participants of the situation change.

The constantly marginal person will form a bridge between two or more points of the social situation: between the formal and informal care system; between citizens and professionals; between the forces of social control and those people who others want to change; between those with resources and those with unmet needs; between citizens given more control over their services and those who control them now. Yet the physical metaphor of the permanent bridge should not be taken too literally. Sometimes the care manager will have to stay in place to link people to each other: to act as a broker of resources. At other times it will be more appropriate for the care manager to link people to each other and then get out of the way and let the relationship develop without professional interference.

It may be the case that no one person in the network can ever be fully marginal in this way, since everyone may necessarily be too involved; in which case it is crucial that the care manager ensures that she gets an approximation to it by ensuring that she hears and synthesises the viewpoint of each member of the network about the whole process, particularly including their perception of the role and behaviour of the care manager.

The evidence

Evidence for the central importance of this broad competency is largely implicit, and framed in different ways. In particular, it is easy to not notice its importance within an individualised model of social problems and service delivery.

Descriptions of the care manager's role in the United States implicitly underline the importance of the care manager being able to work in ways we have characterised as "marginal". For example, in describing the advocacy, service co-ordination and counsellor roles, it is assumed that the worker will have the knowledge and skills necessary to be able to work across boundaries and margins, as described here.

In the development literature emphasis has been placed on the need for workers to draw up area profiles and to understand the patterns of relationships that form the culture, and the needs and resources of their communities. Marginality is identified as a crucial dimension of this work (Smale et al, 1988).

Some evidence for the importance of this broad competency is also found in the PSSRU work. For example:

> "The social worker had however to protect helpers from the risk of over-involvement, which could otherwise lead to their feeling excessively responsible and anxious for the elderly person. This required the worker to provide a framework and the boundaries within which a caring relationship could safely develop". (Challis et al, 1990 p.129)

> "Sometimes in working with carers a great deal of effort had to be put into undoing the original support network and encouraging friends and relatives to withdraw". (Challis et al, 1990 p.47)

Marginality and marginalisation

To actually achieve this order of change in the behaviour of people in the care network, it is clear that the care manager has to have the ability to be appropriately marginal as defined above. This is not the same as being marginalised, which is to be pushed to the fringe of the situation and unable to have any impact on events (Darvill and Smale, 1990).

"Counselling" and beyond

This dimension of the care manager's skills is sometimes assumed in the Gateshead study and elsewhere to be part of "counselling". For example, Challis and colleagues give an example of the process by which a worker simultaneously helps the daughter disengage from her mother, acquires alternative forms of care, and helps the mother change her own expectations and behaviour so as to fit better with the new care arrangements. This complex piece of negotiation with a network of people requires that the worker be able to act as participant, actor and observer in the way defined here as "marginal". However, rather misleadingly, they then go on to say, "Such cases emphasise very clearly the 'direct' work element, such as counselling, in the scheme" (Challis et al, 1990 p. 48).

It is not wrong to describe this process as counselling but it over-simplifies the process of change in a network, the necessity to work with all the people involved, and the essentially "marginal" behaviour of the worker involved relative to the network. In short, intervening in a network to facilitate change requires the strategic competency described here as "marginality".

Challenging: The care manager's ability effectively to confront people with their responsibilities, their problem perpetuating or creating behaviours and their conflicting interests.

Confrontation and empowerment

A crucial dimension of the processes of negotiation that the care manager has to facilitate is the need to challenge particular perceptions, behaviours, and expectations. Such challenging is often a significant dimension of empowerment. For example, Bandana Ahmad has written:

> ". . . avoiding appropriate and necessary social work confrontation is the same as social work inaction, and any social work inaction for Black clients is racist". (Bandana A., 1990 p.35)

The SWIP research into social workers' responses to work with the elderly identified that social workers often:

> ". . . perceived an additional need for counselling, for example, regarding their loneliness, lack of confidence . . . or in coming to terms with serious illness or reduced mobility . . . However, workers often found it difficult to be explicit about this aspect of their assessment and to negotiate an acceptable way of including it in their discussions about needs . . ." (SWIP, 1991 p.5)

Effective challenging

What is implicit here is the need the social worker has to find an effective way of challenging some of the self-perceptions or behaviours of some elderly or other dependent people, carers or other parties to the situation, which may be contributing to the continuance of the problem which brought them to the attention of the social work agency in the first place.

The worker as keeper of resources may also challenge other resource holders, both within their own agency and in others.

There may be many reasons for effective challenging not occurring. The worker may not think it necessary, and may be happy to offer covert counselling; the worker may not be skilled or aware enough; it may be that the worker needs to involve other people in the network; it may be that the worker simply feels that they have not yet developed enough trust and rapport to enable a challenge to be accepted and used by the "client". Though this may be patronising and a chicken-and-egg problem, can trust be developed while important issues are known about and avoided? The development of greater understanding of the need for such challenging behaviour by the care manager, and the development of the concepts and skills required, will be a significant training and educational need in implementing the spirit of community care reforms for a more empowering approach to assessment and care management.

The PSSRU studies clearly underline the importance of the need for the care manager to be able to effectively challenge people in the care network, including the client and staff of the worker's own agency:

> "On other occasions a considerable amount of work was required to assist some reluctant elderly people or families to receive the necessary level of help and to introduce it at a pace which was acceptable to them". (Challis et al, 1990 p.32).

This example can be seen as an illustration of the need for care managers to be able to challenge effectively. The "assisting" of a reluctant dependent person implies that the worker has to get people to change some characteristic patterns of behaviour; to change expectations and attitudes; and to change the way they perceive their responsibilities. In this sense the care manager is having to challenge them. It is important to be more explicit about this than the PSSRU work is, in order to get clearer the nature of the task involved and the micro-skills and strategies which are used.

Advocacy and challenging

The ability to challenge people in the social situation to change their contribution will not only focus on those on the "receiving" end of support. The need for social services professionals to act as advocates has long been established. The research and development work illustrates that workers, and their managers, may have to challenge those who control resources to change their behaviour and decisions, and to pass these skills on to other citizens. Involving users in decisions about how services are to be delivered and planned will challenge those who have traditionally controlled resources, often managers within professional agencies.

Challenging service providers

The care manager will need to be able to challenge the actions of others to hold them to the contracts that contribute services to the "package" of care. Where these are with agencies in the private, not-for-profit or voluntary sector, this may be new territory for social services personnel, but once they are familiar with the new arrangements, it is no more complex than many other business transactions. The care manager may find they carry out their task on much softer ground when the participants in a "package of care" are relatives, friends, neighbours, a community-based self-help group, or other "volunteers". Here they will be operating without the authority of an organisational manager or the financial clout of a purchaser. We will return to this area when we discuss "teamwork" below.

The interplay of skills

We have stressed above that the people involved in the social situation being assessed, the parties to the negotiation of a suitable package of care, will often have different perceptions of problems and their possible solution and often have conflicting interests influencing their choices. The professional has to be able to confront these differences and negotiate a path through them to arrive at a suitable agreement about who will, and can, do what to support whom. The skills of empathy, authenticity and respect are vital elements in being able to helpfully challenge people, as is a capacity to maintain a marginal position.

The inevitability of painful decisions

We have stressed that the new language of community care and a shift to market transactions to purchase services should not deceive anybody into thinking that assessment and care management are as simple as shopping in the supermarket. The most common, and often the most difficult situations in which the professional will have to call upon their skill to challenge others, will not come from disagreements with them: they will come from having to confront the feelings aroused by different people's needs and choices coming out into the open. Painful decisions have to be made and people will often not be able to have what they want, sometimes through lack of resources, sometimes because their needs conflict with others, sometimes through irretrievable loss of a person or personal capacity and often through some combination of all of these factors.

Popularity is not necessarily one of the core attributes of the empowering assessor and care manager.

Conceptualisation: The care manager's ability to pattern, or make sense of, data, in whatever form presented.

The task of assessing the social situations which typically confront staff of social services and social work agencies is often complex. This complexity will increase with the emphasis on user and carer involvement, and the need to understand and negotiate across often large and fluid networks of people and to achieve collaboration with different agencies. It is always possible to oversimplify situations for the purpose of administrative and bureaucratic convenience, but to do so goes against the spirit of the reforms, and anyway will always doom the worker to ineffectiveness. Consequently, it becomes essential that the care manager is able to conceptualise, that is pattern or make sense of all the data available. This will be very varied: it will include hard facts, and also the expression of personal feeling; it will include knowledge about this particular family obtained from another agency, but also more general knowledge about the community in which they live.

The role of theory

What knowledge is seen as relevant, and how it is used in planning, will be determined by implicit and explicit theories held by the worker and should be guided by what the other people involved regard as pertinent. This in itself may well be contested within the networks of people involved; hence the care manager will need to be able to make sense of the ways other people perceive the situation, and use this knowledge appropriately. In Part One we distinguished between the Exchange, Questioning and Procedural models. Where the latter is the main form of assessment, then "theory" may be dictated by agency criteria for eligibility for service provision. If service eligibility is the only criterion, then workers may not be concerned to contribute to the management of the person's care, and so their interest in who does what for whom and how this might change, will be limited. But such an approach is more constant with a service led approach than one which is designed to increase people's choices.

"Administrative" and "complete" case management

Elsewhere a distinction has been made between "administrative" and "complete" care management. Of the latter, Challis and colleagues write that it ranges from:

> ". . . at the lowest level, situations where objectives are clearly prescribed—as the allocation and provision of one service— where both ends and means are specified; through, at a second level, situations where both ends and means are less clear, requiring broad-ranging assessments to decide on ends and decisions about possible solutions; to a third level, situations where new types of response have to be created since again ends are unclear, requiring broad-ranging assessments, and suitable means do not exist, requiring not just decisions choosing between possible solutions but also the creation of new services or responses. The care management role is one which spans each of these different levels." (Challis et al, 1990 p.15)

Including all dimensions

To such complexity it is necessary to add that conceptualisation must always include the worker's behaviour and that of others in his or her own agency. Conceptualisation is not just the process of thinking "objectively" about the "client" and their social circumstances; it is a part of the wider process of negotiation in which how the worker is thinking needs to be included in the overall pattern. For example, the SWIP research identified a number of cases in which:

> ". . . workers sometimes based their actions on their own professional assessment of the client's needs without sharing this assessment with the client. This could be extremely puzzling for the client . . . This approach, far from countering dependency, actually bolsters what Phillipson terms the 'structured dependency of the elderly' through the construction of dependency creating relationships." (SWIP, 1991 p.5)

Clearly, with such processes being possible, in which the behaviour of the worker may actually be exacerbating the initial problem, it becomes crucial that the worker's own behaviour and that of other staff in the agency become part of the process which is patterned and conceptualised.

Conceptualisation and stereotyping

There is a continuing risk that the process of assessment becomes a more or less sophisticated form of stereotyping. The move towards a "needs-led" approach can be seen as an attempt to prevent the stereotyping which is inevitable within a "service-led" approach. It is inevitable some people have to be viewed simply in accordance with the very limited categories the organisation creates for dividing up its services. The needs-led approach offers a choice to prevent this, but does not guarantee it. It will still be possible for the care manager to view the "needs" of a dependent person, their carers and others through to a particular set of stereotypical assumptions. This is particularly likely if the care manager is well versed in research on "the needs of elderly people", for example, since this general knowledge will have a general "objective" reliability.

"Testing" not "applying" theory

What is necessary is for the care manager to conceptualise, or theorise afresh in each situation: not by ignoring available knowledge, but by clearly making such knowledge of population and groups a guide to thinking about a particular situation, and not its leader. Each new situation should be seen as an opportunity actively to **test** the fallibility of existing theory and knowledge, and not just as an opportunity to avoid the effort of thinking by "applying" existing certitudes. This is a major dimension of reinventing practice to meet each new social situation; of tailor making services.

Reframing: The care manager's ability to help redefine circumstances in ways which lead towards problem resolution.

Problem definition and resolution

Social care agencies often get drawn into situations in which the problem is being defined in ways which preclude it being resolved. Most people, as argued previously, are cared for by themselves and others in their own social and family networks without becoming a "social problem". When they are referred it is often at a point of crisis, and when people feel that they "cannot cope any more". In these circumstance the process of assessment, the negotiations between members of the person's network, the care manager and others, may well require some reframing of perceptions of the problem so that it becomes perceived as more solvable.

The evidence

There is a great deal of literature on creativity and the nature of social and interpersonal problem-solving, all of which includes some concept of "reframing": of helping people get a different perspective or fresh definition of the situation in which they are "stuck". This literature is very diverse, and includes work from communications theory; family therapy; organisation theory and management theory (Watzlawick et al, 1974; Egan, 1985, 1990; Goldstein, 1984; Peters, 1988; Henry, 1991; Morgan, 1989).

Levels of reframing

Reframing may be necessary at many different levels, not just the individual service provision level. For example, the development of the Health and Social Care pilot project in Gateshead can be seen as involving a measure of reframing. Certain user needs were not being met by the existing scheme, and what was initially framed as a "client problem"—certain client needs not being met—was reframed as a problem in the way the different agencies addressing this were organised. Consequently, a new interagency team was developed which handled the initial client problems better.

*"Problem" or
"stress"?*

The SWIP research describes how workers have to be particularly careful about the manner in which they offer counselling. Carers may be uncomfortable with the view that their stress is a "problem", and hence may reject help with this. However, a more tacit acknowledgement of this stress, that is a framing of it as such, as against framing it as a "problem", makes the offer of help, and hence resolution of part of the problem, more likely. They write:

> "Social Work in Partnership found that a tacit agreement of this nature 'allows for the issue of personal support for the carer to be legitimately on the agenda without the carer explicitly having to acknowledge and name this as a problem for which service is sought'". (SWIP, 1991 p.6)

Arranging, Maintaining and Rearranging

Social care planning: The care manager's ability to contribute towards understanding and systematically planning responses to patterns of behaviour which precipitate and perpetuate social problems in all kinds of social networks.

Levels of planning

Social care planning in the sense defined has to occur at several levels. Care managers need to be able to inform and influence the processes by which "community care plans" are developed in their areas, and to do this in partnership with users, carers and local citizens generally. The care manager's experience of planning and facilitating "packages of care" with individuals, families and other people in local communities needs to inform such planning and development processes.

Community care and social care

There is a danger that the thinking and planning for the implementation of the NHS and Community Care and the Children Acts reforms become split from each other when it has been made explicit in government thinking that the two reforms are to be seen as consistent and complementary. This implies that the "community care plans" which local authorities have to prepare are best understood as part of "social care plans" that incorporate plans for both children's services and those for other user groups. (Smale et al, 1992)

Planning from the bottom up

Such social care plans need to be built from the bottom up by bringing together knowledge developed through partnerships with local people, community groups and voluntary organisations as well as the knowledge gained by care managers and their teams through their direct work with individuals, families and other people involved in forming packages of care.

For the social care plans (or community care plans) at the departmental level to be accurate, and to be the product of genuine partnership with citizens, be they direct users of services, carers or others, they need to be an aggregate of the kinds of local information which the care manager and her team colleagues have to be developing anyway. The indirect work discussed previously, which is necessary in order to develop resources in the community which do not already exist, and to change the way resources are currently deployed, both requires and helps create the kind of local knowledge crucial to the wider planning process. The care manager's contribution to this wider planning process is also, of course, a dimension of the indirect work which is also necessary in order to help create the resources necessary for some of the direct work of creating individual packages of care. The care manager has a pivotal role in contributing to the communication networks necessary to link these different planning and development levels.

The care manager's pivotal role

If we consider the story of the Smith family, the very existence of the lunch club, run by a local voluntary organisation, and financially supported by the local authority social services department, is a product of a complex local social care planning process in which a worker in the role of care manager may have played a significant part. For example, in influencing the social services committee to commit funding, the care manager may have prepared a report jointly with local members of the voluntary organisation and people in the locality who would be potential users. This report, reinforced by local statistical information and "area profiles" and supported by several case examples drawn from the team's direct work, would constitute the care manager's contribution both to local social care planning, and the more strategic planning processes.

This planning needs to be ongoing. For example, the Smith family may be members of a particular minority ethnic group with special dietary requirements which require some changes in the kinds of menu offered by the lunch club. The care manager, noticing this, might encourage wider recognition of such needs in the community which sets in train other developments both in relation to that particular lunch club, or possibly the development of a quite new service in the area.

Planning as a synthesising competency

The activities which make up social care planning are diverse, but the most basic skills which underlie these activities are identical to those required for an empowering approach to assessment and care management generally. To engage in processes of social care planning in partnership with others requires the care manager to really listen to others, and to share with them her understanding of their situation. It requires an ability to pattern, and make sense of complex information of many different kinds; it requires respect for others, and respect for the way they currently handle difficulties and so on. In this sense social care planning can be understood as a major synthesising competency required of the care manager at all levels of their work.

The evidence

The SWIP research and work done on Black perspectives reinforces the importance of this wider approach to social care planning. For example:
> "The assessment of need is a complex task which cannot be reduced to simple formulas such as, for example, dependency/ independence . . . A number of social workers, for example, could not see the point of joint negotiation about needs and

goals in 'routine' assessments for residential care". (SWIP, 1991 p.2)

Routine, service-led "assessments" are the antithesis of an empowering approach to assessment and care management which will only be possible if staff develop the core skills and attitudes involved in social care planning as characterised above. Further discussion of the need for such approaches to social care planning, and practice illustrations are to be found in, for example, Darvill and Smale, 1990; Crosbie and Vickery, 1989; Smale and Bennett, 1989; Sinclair et al, 1990.

This extended and integrated vision of social care planning is widely argued for within discussions about services for minority ethnic communities. For example Arshi Ahmad writes:
"Assessing a client's eligibility for services is often not done on the basis of needs, but on whether the needs comply with the criteria for service provision laid down by the social services department . . . For example, the criteria for home care may exclude those elderly people who have other (younger) family members living in the same accommodation. Less priority is given to clients who appear to have family members to care for them. Black people may be more likely than white elderly people to live in shared accommodation with younger members of the family. This illustrates the way in which assessment processes exclude Black people from receiving an effective or equitable service." (Ahmad A., 1990 p.32)

The more complex, holistic and integrated approach to assessment and care management, essential if such discrimination is to be avoided and promoted in the spirit of the legislation, will require the synthesising skills of social care planning as defined.

Guarding against colonisation

Much stress has been placed on the need for social services departments to be committed to learning the views of the people they serve, citizens such as Mrs Smith, Rose and Tom. They will need to be informed and included in reviews of existing and possible future services and views of people like them built into the policy and planning process (Jowell, 1987). In planning new services it will be necessary to guard against the colonisation of the voluntary sector (Bulmer, 1986) and to recognise that the purchaser-provider relationships could undermine the essential advocate role of some local groups and voluntary organisations. This has been identified as a particular problem for the Black and minority ethnic community groups (Jones, 1991).

Collaboration within the community

But collaboration with people in the community to plan services is a necessary but not sufficient move towards empowerment of citizens to exercise choice over their services. There is a growing body of practice experience to illustrate how people in Mrs Smith, Rose and Tom's position can become members of the management team running their services (Croft and Beresford, 1990; Smale and Bennett, 1989; Darvill and Smale, 1990; Smale et al, 1992). Given the opportunities, support and information, participation at this level becomes possible, making services more relevant and sharing control with all involved.

Partnership: The care manager's ability to negotiate, carry out and review collaborative working and management practice with whoever is necessary.

It has been stated that the skills described above are overlapping attributes. Just as social care planning needs a synthesis of some of these skills so they come together in the ability of professionals to work in partnership with those citizens who receive and give care to others and in their collaboration with other professionals: the people who work in different agencies and professional groups.

Ensuring involvement

The ability to work effectively as initiator, guide, and/or member of different kinds of team is an essential requirement of the care manager, as is their ability to work in partnership with others through understanding, using and developing many different kinds of informal networks. It has been stressed that a package of care is essentially a fluid set of human relationships, a set of different kinds of partnerships, to which the care manager has to make an appropriate and flexible contribution. Social care planning has to be a process in which users, carers and others in the community and professional networks are given maximum opportunity for involvement and partnership. The care manager has a significant role in ensuring, facilitating and maintaining such involvements.

Participative management and local partnerships

For the care manager to initiate and develop partnerships with users, community groups and others at the local level requires that the care manager works in a context of participative management since the task requires the care manager to have sufficient delegated responsibility to be able to form all the partnerships required for all levels of the work. Research reviewed in the companion to this report draws attention to the common failure to translate joint planning at the organisational level to working partnerships at the local level, and hence the development of local partnerships has to be seen as a major task in its own right, and one in which the care manager has to have a major role. (Smale et al, 1992)

Devolved decision-making

With the Smith family, for example, the care manager needs to be able to decide for herself, using her own professional judgment in partnership with her colleagues, members of the family and people in the wider social context, about what changes may be possible, what direct services might be made available, what the next steps of the care manager herself might be, etc. If she has continually to refer to someone higher in her hierarchy, who in turn has to do the same thing, then a split opens up between those who actually know most about the situation on the ground, and those who are making key decisions. This will inevitably be disempowering for the user and others involved with the dependent person. Partnership thus requires, and is encouraged by, devolution of decision-making as close to the team of people actually tackling the problem as possible. This will in turn model the devolution of decision-making which the care manager herself has to encourage in her partnerships with users, carers and others in the community. Where this does not take place, the involvement of citizens in planning and managing their services can lead to conflict and disillusionment. (Smale and Bennett, 1989)

Teamwork

The necessity for "teamwork" within the organisation, between staff from different agencies, and between professionals and citizens, has been stressed as a major implication of community-based practice, research and development work for the implementation of the reforms. (Smale et al, 1992)

The evidence

Serious consideration has to be given to building a "team" of compatible members to constitute the "care package" or "care network". The perceptions and attitudes of "users" and "carers" have to be given due weight by the care manager in the building and maintenance of the team since they are central members of it. This approach to the necessity of including users and others in the "team" is supported by the SWIP research. For example:

> ". . . if genuine participation is to underpin the new approach to service provision assessment must become a process of working alongside people in recognition of the fact that, as the SSI states, 'some users may be the best assessors of their own needs and solutions'". (SWIP, 1991 p.2)

If **users** are the best assessors of their own needs then clearly they **need to be viewed as members of the team involved in assessment and care management.** This is a particularly pressing issue in relation to work with minority ethnic groups where there has been a pattern of exclusion of user and carer involvement in the assessment of needs and the formulation of a package of response. For example, Bandana Ahmad argues in *Black Perspectives in Social Work* that improvements in social work with Black communities will require, among other things, that staff:

> "Engage Black client systems in social work problem solving by 'recognising' and 'utilising' the strengths of Black families and their communities . . . Increase Black clients' power by ensuring that they have information and knowledge of services, resources, entitlements, choices etc., and linking them with those agencies, support networks, campaign groups, professionals etc. who are engaged in combating social inequality and injustice." (Ahmad, B., 1990 pp.47–48)

The PSSRU research in Gateshead and Kent clearly underlines the central importance of partnerships, rather than the individual worker, as the unit which undertakes the work of assessment and care management. The two care management projects studied were essentially team projects. The different projects involved different kinds of "team", but this difference underlines both the ubiquity and the variety of partnerships necessary. The full implications of this are not completely explicit in the PSSRU work, but the evidence is there. For example:

> "In considering who would best relate to a particular elderly person, attention was paid to factors such as personality, attitudes . . . in addition to obvious features such as availability and geographical proximity." (Challis et al, 1990 p.125)

The centrality of partnership, and particularly the extension of the idea of teamwork to include users, carers, and staff from other agencies and the voluntary sector is supported by wider literature on collaboration in community care (Gibbons, 1990; Bayley et al, 1989; Crosbie and Vickery, 1989).

Facilitating renegotiation of team membership

As with any partnership, it requires the care manager to facilitate continuous re-negotiation with members of the team or care network about different perceptions of purposes, resources, conflicting interests, conflicting views about who does what in the "team" etc. For example, Challis and colleagues write:

> "Perceptions of what was tolerable differed between families, agencies and indeed social services staff themselves. The care manager was required to hold a clear conception of what constituted acceptable risk for a given individual and to work to achieve a balance between the views of others and the rights of the elderly person". (Challis et al, 1990 p.31)

This enabling and facilitating role draws upon all the other strategic skills identified elsewhere in this section, as well as those traditionally, and more widely, associated with the coordination of teams and groups. Many of the skills required of the care manager as identified by the PSSRU research in Gateshead and elsewhere support this. For example:

> "Resolve conflict between client, family and services.
> Formulate the care plan and clarify with all parties involved.
> Mobilise client's informal network of support.
> Ensure that all services contribute effectively to the overall care plan . . ." (Challis et al, 1990 p.9)

Learning tasks for care management staff

The ability to develop teams, engage in network linking and the leadership skills essential for conflict resolution, and network mobilisations and so forth will be major learning tasks for staff involved in care management. New approaches to thinking about teams and teamwork will be necessary in order to accommodate the flexible, fluid, and often transitory nature of the teams.

It has been stressed that the ability to develop flexible and diverse partnerships will draw upon the whole range of competencies already discussed. To join with others is to form partnerships, and to do this successfully requires the care manager to be honest and straight with people, so that members of the partnership really do know where they stand with each other. The explicit initiation of partnerships with networks of people who are already in relationship, such as members of a community group or family, may require considerable thought and reflection. The ways people in such groups and networks relate to each other will often have developed over many years. The care manager may have to use their skills of empathy and understanding of the patterns of relationship to catch up with the intuitive shared understandings which the existing members already have. The skill of forming effective partnerships is thus a complex synthesising skill which will draw upon all the existing social skill and knowledge of the care manager.

Conclusions

In this short report we have attempted to address two questions:

- How can the professional carry out assessments and care management so as to maximise the choice of the major parties, i.e. to empower people?

- What skills do workers need to put such an approach into practice?

The work has been carried out in parallel with a review of research and development work on community based practice. Three models for describing different approaches to the task have been described and their relationship to empowerment discussed. We have stressed the need for:

- **the social situation to be the focus of assessments and subsequent care management activity;**

- **recognition that the dependability of people in the community is as crucial as the dependency needs of particular individuals;**

- **the assessment and care management team to be involved in the development of local resources as well as tackling problems at the level of individuals and their personal networks.**

To be helpful to workers we would like to have set out a simple, easy approach to assessment and care management with clear guidelines for them to follow. But the task is not simple. Assessments will often be made at crucial stages in people's lives when they are confronted with the major issues of living, dying and relating to others. To engage fully with people at such times, professionals have to be able to join with them and struggle with complexity. They will have to be able to act with skill and sensitivity if they are to introduce resources to increase people's choices without taking away some of the control that people have over their lives.

In Part Two we have described the areas of skill and knowledge required for such work. Further work will be needed to develop appropriate staff development methods and materials to educate and train staff to carry out these tasks. This is particularly true if the change in attitude advocated throughout the reforms is to be made and put into practice. The approach to practice and management described here is a form of "reflective practice" and as such requires training and staff development that is based on "coaching" and experiential learning involving "enactment" rather than didactic teaching and simulated learning experiences (Argyris, 1982; Schon 1983, 1987; Smale, 1987; Smale and Tuson, 1988).

For workers to promote user choice by sharing decision making with them will also have implications for their own management and professional supervision.

This whole approach is based on an awareness that:

- the bulk of care in the community is, and is likely to remain, the responsibility and task of ordinary citizens;

- but a small percentage of people are entirely dependent on professional social services, and for others, a little help makes a huge difference.

Many of the people who normally care for those dependent on others, choose to do what they do, but if realistically asked would probably not choose to do quite so much. Improving community care and extending it to a growing population of potential recipients will depend upon developing the skill and vision of the professionals concerned and enabling them to work in partnership with people to develop the resources in the community that normally meet people's needs. Of all the resources required for community care, this remains a crucial area of investment.

References

Ahmad, A. (1990) *Practice with Care*. London: Race Equality Unit, National Institute for Social Work.

Ahmad, B. (1990) *Black Perspectives in Social Work*. Birmingham: Venture Press for Race Equality Unit, National Institute for Social Work.

Avon County Council (1980) *Admissions to Homes for the Elderly*. Avon County Council, Social Services Department.

Barclay, P.M. (Chmn.) (1982) *Social Workers: Their Role and Tasks. The report of a working party*. London: Bedford Square Press for National Institute for Social Work.

Barkham, M. (1988) Empathy in counselling and psychotherapy: present status and future directions. *Counselling Psychology Quarterly* Vol.1, No.4.

Bayley, M. Seyd, R. and Tennant, A. (1989) *Local Health and Welfare*. London: Unwin Hyman.

Bebbington, A. and Tong, M. (1986) Trends and changes in old people's homes: provision over twenty years. In Judge, K. and Sinclair, I. (eds.) *Residential Care for Elderly People*. London: HMSO.

Berry, L. (1990) *Information for Users of Social Services Departments*. London: National Consumer Council/National Institute for Social Work

Biehal, N. (1991) Participation in decision making: defining needs and making choices. Unpublished discussion paper.

Booth, T.A. Barritt, S. Berry, S. Martin, D. N. and Melotte, C. (1983) *A Follow-up Study of the Trends in Dependency in Local Authority Homes for the Elderly 1980–82*. Sheffield: JUSSR, University of Sheffield.

Bowling, A.C. and Bleatham, C. (1982) The need for nursing and other skilled care in local authority residential homes for the elderly: research report no.5. *Clearing House for Local Authority Social Services Research* (9), pp.1–65. Birmingham: Birmingham University.

Bricker-Jenkins, M. (1990) Another approach to practice and training—clients must be considered the primary experts. *Public Welfare*, Spring, pp.11–16.

Bulmer, M. (1986) *Neighbours: the Work of Philip Abrams*. Cambridge: Cambridge University Press.

Bulmer, M. (1987) *The Social Basis of Community Care*. London: Unwin Hyman.

Carkhuff, R.R. (1971) *The Development of Human Resources: Education, Psychology and Social Change*. New York: Holt, Reinhart and Winston Inc.

Challis, D. and Davies, B. (1986) *Case Management in Community Care*. Aldershot: Gower Publishing Company.

Challis, D. et al (1990) *Case Management in Social and Health Care*. Canterbury: University of Kent Personal Social Services Research Unit.

Croft, S. and Beresford, P. (1990) *From Paternalism to Participation: Involving People in Social Services* London: Open Services Project.

Crosbie, D. and Vickery, A. (1989) *Community Based Schemes in Area Offices*. Report to the Department of Health. London: National Institute for Social Work.

Darvill, G. and Smale, G. (eds.) (1990) *Partners in Empowerment: Networks of Innovation in Social Work*. (Pictures of Practice, Vol. II). London: National Institute for Social Work.

Department of Health and Social Security (1985) *Social Work Decisions in Child Care: Recent Research Findings and their Implications*. London: HMSO.

Department of Health (1989) *Caring for People: Community Care in the Next Decade and Beyond*. (CM 849) London: HMSO.

Department of Health: Social Services Inspectorate (1991) *Getting the Message Across: A Guide to Developing and Communicating Policies, Principles and Procedures on Assessment*. London: HMSO.

Doel, M. and Marsh, P. (1992) *Task-Centred Social Work*. London: Ashgate.

Egan, G. (1985) *Change Agent Skills in Helping and Human Service Settings*. California, USA: Brooks Cole Belmont.

Egan, G. (1990) *The Skilled Helper: A Systematic Approach to Effective Helping*. 4th Edition. California, USA: Brooks Cole Belmont.

Elliott (1985) Helpful and non-helpful events in brief counselling interviews: an empirical taxonomy. *Journal of Counselling Psychology* (32), pp. 307–332.

Family Law Review (1987) (1), pp. 269–347.

Finch, J. and Groves, D. (1983) *Labour of Love*. London: Routledge and Kegan Paul.

Fisher, M., Marsh, P. and Phillips, D. with Sainsbury, E. (1986) *In and Out of Care: The Experience of Children, Parents and Social Workers*. London: Batsford.

Fisher, M. (1990) *Care Management and Social Work: Working with Carers*. Bradford: University of Bradford.

Fortune, A.E. (ed.) (1985) *Task-Centred Practice with Families and Groups*. New York: Springer Publishing Company.

Freire, P. (1972) *Pedagogy of the Oppressed*. Harmondsworth: Penguin Books.

Gibbons, J. (1990) *Family Support and Prevention: Studies in Local Areas.* London: HMSO.

Goldstein, H.(ed.) (1984) *Creative Change: A Cognitive-Humanistic Approach to Social Work Practice.* London: Tavistock.

Green, H. (1988) *Informal Carers: General Household Survey, 1985.* London: HMSO.

Griffiths, R. (1988) *Community Care: Agenda for Action. A report to the secretary of state for social services.* London: HMSO.

Gurman, A.S. and Kniskern, D.P. (1978) Research on marital and family therapy: Progress, perspective and prospect. In Garfield, S. and Bergin, A. *Handbook of Psychotherapy and Behaviour Change* 2nd Edition. New York: John Wiley.

Hadley, R. and McGrath, M. (1984) *When Social Services are Local: The Normanton Experience.* London: Allen and Unwin.

Hadley, R. et al (1984) *Decentralising Social Services: A Model for Change.* London: Bedford Square Press.

Hadley, R. et al (1987) *A Community Social Worker's Handbook.* London: Tavistock.

Harre, R. (1980) *Social Being.* Littlefield: Adams.

Henry, J. (ed.) (1991) *Creative Management.* London: Sage.

Higbee, M., Dukes, G. and Bosso, J. (1982) Patient recall of physician's prescription instructions. *Hospital Formulary* (17), pp. 553–556.

Jones, A (1991) *Black Community Care: Report of the Black Communities Care Project.* Leeds: National Institute for Social Work.

Jowell, T. (1987) *Project Journal*, first edition. Community Care Special Action Project, Birmingham City Council.

Levin E. (1991) *Carers—Problems, Strains and Services.* London: National Institute for Social Work.

Levin, E., Sinclair, I. and Gorbach, P. (1989) *Families, Services and Confusion in Old Age.* Aldershot: Avebury

Macdevitt (1987) Therapists' personal therapy and professional self-awareness. *Psychotherapy* (24), pp. 693–703.

Marsh, P. and Fisher, M. (1992) *Good Intentions: Developing Partnership in Social Services.* York: Joseph Rowntree Foundation.

Meichenbaum, D. and Turk, D.C. (1987) *Facilitating Treatment Adherence—A Practitioner's Guidebook.* New York: Plenum Press.

Miller, C., Crosbie, D. and Vickery, A. (1991) *Everyday Community Care: A Manual for Managers.* London: National Institute for Social Work.

Minuchin, S. and Fisman, C.H. (1981) *Family Therapy Techniques.* Harvard, USA: Harvard University Press.

Morgan, G. (1989) *Creative Organisation Theory.* London: Sage.

Morrison, C. (1988) Consumerism—lessons from community work. *Public Administration* (66), Summer, pp. 205–214.

Neill, J. Sinclair, I. Gorbach, P. and Williams, J. (1988) *A Need For Care? Elderly Applicants for Local Authority Homes.* Aldershot: Avebury.

Norcross, J. Strausser, D.J. and Faltus, F.J. (1988) The therapist's therapist. *American Journal of Psychotherapy* (42), pp. 53–66.

Parker, G. (1985) *With Due Care and Attention: A Review of Research on Informal Care.* Occasional Paper No. 2. London: Family Policy Studies Centre.

Patterson, C.H. (1984) Empathy, warmth and genuineness in psychotherapy. *Psychotherapy* Vol. 21 No.4.

Peters, T. (1988) *Thriving on Chaos:Handbook for a Management Revolution.* London: Macmillan.

Phillipson, C. (1989) Challenging dependency: towards a new social work with older people. In Langan, M. and Lee, P. *Radical Social Work Today.* London: Unwin Hyman.

Potter, J. (1988) Consumerism and the public sector: how well does the cost fit? *Public Administration* (66), Summer, pp.149–164.

Power, M., Clough, D., Gibson, P. and Kelly, S. (1983) *Helping Lively Minds: Volunteer Support to Residential Homes.* Bristol: University of Bristol

Raines, J.C. (1990) Empathy in clinical social work. *Clinical Social Work Journal.* Vol. 18 No. 1.

Reid, W.J. (1987) *Family Problem Solving.* New York: Columbia University Press.

Roger, C. (1986) Reflection of feelings. *Person-Centred Review* (2), pp. 375–377.

Rogers, E. (1983) *The Diffusion of Innovations* Third Edition New York: The Free Press.

Rogers, E. and Kincaid, D.L. (1981) *Communications Networks: Toward a New Paradigm for Research* New York: The Free Press.

Seyd, R., Tennant, A., Bayley, M., and Parker, P. (1984) *Community Social Work.* Sheffield: University of Sheffield.

Shapiro, D. and Shapiro, D. (1987) Change Processes in Psychotherapy. *British Journal and Addiction* Vol. 82 No. 4.

SHARPEN (1984) *Scottish Health Authorities Review of Priorities for the Eighties and Nineties.*

Shaull, R. (1972) Foreword to Friere, *Pedagogy of the Oppressed.* Harmondsworth: Penguin Books.

Shaw, I. and Walton, R. (1979) Transitions to residence in homes for the elderly. In Harris, D. and Hyland, J. (eds.) *Rights in Residence.* London: RCA.

Sinclair, I., Crosbie, D., O'Conner, P., Stanforth, L. and Vickery, A. (1988) *Bridging Two Worlds: Social Work and the Elderly Living Alone.* Aldershot: Gower.

Sinclair, I. Parker, R. Leat, D. and Williams, J. (1990) *The Kaleidoscope of Care: A Review of Research on Welfare Provision for Elderly People.* London: HMSO for National Institute for Social Work.

Smale, G. (1983) Can we afford not to develop social work practice? *British Journal of Social Work* (13) pp. 251–264.

Smale, G. (1987) Some principles of interactional skills training. *Social Work Education*. Vol. 7 No. 1.

Smale, G. (1991) *Developing Models of Empowerment and Practice Theory.* Unpublished discussion paper. Practice and Development Exchange: National Institute for Social Work.

Smale, G. and Bennett, W. (1989) *Pictures of Practice: Volume I. Community Social Work in Scotland.* London: National Institute for Social Work.

Smale, G. and Tuson, G. (1988) *Learning for Change.* London: National Institute for Social Work.

Smale, G. Tuson, G. Cooper, M. Wardle, M. and Crosbie, D. (1988) *Community Social Work: A Paradigm for Change.* London: National Institute for Social Work.

Smale, G. and Tuson, G. with Biehal, N. and Marsh, P. (1992) *Negotiating Care in the Community.* The implications of research findings on community based practice for the implementation of the NHS and Community Care and the Children Acts. London: National Institute for Social Work.

Smith, P.B. Wood, H. and Smale, G. (1980) The usefulness of groups. In Smith, P.B. (ed.) *Small Groups and Personal Change.* London: Methuen.

Stapleton, B. (1976) *A Survey of the Waiting List for Places in Newham's Hostels for the Elderly.* London Borough of Newham, Applied Research Section.

SWIP Research Paper (1991) *Follow-up Interviews: Data Analysis.* Unpublished. Sheffield: University of Sheffield.

Townsend, P. (1962) *The Last Refuge.* London: Routledge and Kegan Paul.

Wade, B. Sawyer, L. and Bell, S. (1983) *Dependency with Dignity.* London: Bedford Square Press.

Wagner Committee (1988) *Residential Care: A Positive Choice.* Report of the independent review of residential care, chaired by Gillian Wagner. London: HMSO.

Watzlawick, P. Weak, J. and Fisch, R. (1974) *Change: Principles of Problem Formation and Problem Resolution.* New York: Norton.

Whitehead (1929) *Aims of Education.* London: MacMillan.

Whittaker, J. (1986) Integrating formal and informal social care: a conceptual framework. *British Journal of Social Work* (16) Supplement, pp.39–62.

Willcocks, D. Peace, S. Kellaher, L. and Ring, J. (1982) *The Residential Life of Old People.* London: Survey Research Unit, Polytechnic of North London.

Wodarski, J. and Bagarozzi, D. (1979) A review of the empirical status of traditional modes of interpersonal helping: implications for social work practice. *Clinical Social Work Journal* pp. 231–254.

Wootton, B. (1959) *Social Science and Social Pathology.* London: Allen and Unwin.

Empowering Users to make Choices: Assessment, Care Management and the Skilled Worker

This report was commissioned by the Department of Health, in the light of the implications of implementing the NHS and Community Care and the Children Acts, to look at:

- the skills required by social services staff for assessment and care management;

- how to ensure users are empowered to participate in the choices made about addressing their needs;

- how to involve members of users' social networks in arrangements integrating resources from the statutory and independent sectors.

The report begins with a discussion of the core skills required and the underlying principles, drawn from the authors' experience of developing community based practice in partnership with local people (projects at the National Institute for Social Work, and Sheffield and Bradford Universities). The focus is on making face-to-face contacts with members of the public to plan services, as a first step in the process.

Part One addresses a framework for empowering people to participate, the principles underlying partnership, and the relationship between care management and empowerment.

Part Two describes the core skills identified in the research and development literature on community-based approaches to social work practice and service delivery.

The conclusion emphasises that improving community care and extending it depends on developing the skills and vision of the professionals concerned, thus enabling them to build on the resources of local communities.

HMSO details/price

Printed in the United Kingdom for HMSO
Dd295536 1/93 C40 G531 10170